Mini-Book of the Week

❋❋❋❋❋❋❋❋

by Maria Fleming

NEW YORK · TORONTO · LONDON · AUCKLAND · SYDNEY
MEXICO CITY · NEW DELHI · HONG KONG · BUENOS AIRES

Teaching *Resources*

Cover design by Jim Sarfati

Cover illustrations by Anne Kennedy

Interior design by Sydney Wright

Interior illustrations by Anne Kennedy (pages 11-15, 26-29, 32-41, 51-53, 56-57, 66-68, 72-73, 78-79, 85-88, 93-96)
and Maxie Chambliss (16-25, 30-31, 42-50, 54-55, 58-65, 69-71, 74-77, 80-84, 89-91)

ISBN: 0-439-05921-6

Copyright © 2005 by Maria Fleming

Published by Scholastic Inc.

5 6 7 8 9 10   40   13 12 11 10 09 08 07 06

Contents

Introduction

Welcome to *Mini-Book of the Week*—a great way to put a new book in the hands of every student, every week of the school year! Inside are reproducible patterns to make 40 fiction and nonfiction mini-books that commemorate holidays and special occasions, celebrate seasonal changes, and explore favorite themes, all while providing valuable reading practice and reinforcing key concepts. Many of the books feature fun formats—such as flip books, shape books, pop-up books, interactive write-and-read books, and more—that motivate children to read them again and again. Young readers will be eager to bring home these books to share with family members, helping to build students' reading confidence and skills.

Looking for a fun way to mark the arrival of fall? Try the mini-book "Leaf Walk," which invites children to notice the different shapes of leaves. Need to find an engaging reading and math activity to incorporate into your 100th Day of School celebration? Turn to the mini-book "How Do You Count to 100?" which gives children practice counting 100 critters. Want to wrap up the school year on a positive note? Invite children to write and illustrate their own "Class Memory Book" to show their special memories of the year. From the first day of school to the last, these mini-books provide lots of engaging reading practice.

You'll find no end to the uses of these little books. Here are some suggestions. Use the books

- ☺ to introduce or reinforce a specific reading skill.
- ☺ to teach guided reading lessons.
- ☺ to compare fiction and nonfiction.
- ☺ to launch a theme unit.
- ☺ to reinforce science, social studies, and math content.
- ☺ to give children practice reading in a learning center or in a listening center with a recording of the text.
- ☺ to provide a model for children's creative writing and bookmaking projects.
- ☺ to build personal mini-book libraries for every student.

And most importantly, use the books to inspire a love of reading and reinforce the idea that reading is fun—something to be enjoyed every day, every week, and every season of the year!

Connections to the Language Arts Standards

The activities in this book are designed to support you in meeting the following reading standards outlined by Mid-continent Research for Education and Learning, an organization that collects and synthesizes national and state K–12 curriculum standards.

- ❋ Uses mental images based on pictures and print to aid in comprehension of text
- ❋ Uses meaning clues to aid comprehension and make predictions about content
- ❋ Uses basic elements of phonetic analysis to decode unknown words
- ❋ Understands level-appropriate sight words and vocabulary
- ❋ Uses self-correction strategies
- ❋ Reads aloud familiar stories with fluency and expression
- ❋ Uses reading skills and strategies to understand a variety of familiar literary passages and texts (folktales, fiction, nonfiction, poems, picture books, predictable books)
- ❋ Uses reading skills and strategies to understand a variety of informational texts
- ❋ Understands the main idea and supporting details of simple expository information

Source—*Content Knowledge: A Compendium of Standards and Benchmarks for K–12 Education* (4th ed.) (Mid-continent Research for Education and Learning, 2000)

How to Make the Mini-Books

For standard format mini-books, follow the assembly instructions below. For other formats, follow the instructions in this section listed by title.

Tips for All Mini-Books:

• Carefully remove the mini-book pages along the perforated lines.

• Make photocopies of the book pages on 8½- by 11-inch paper. All books except for "The Seasons of an Apple Tree" (October, Week 1) require single-sided photocopies. Feed the pages into the photocopier with one one of the short sides first.

• For quicker assembly of shape books, cut the pages apart along the dotted lines instead of cutting out the shapes.

Assembly Instructions for Standard Format Mini-Books

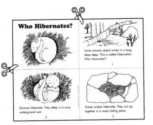

1. Make single-sided photocopies of the book pages.

2. Cut apart the mini-book pages.

3. Stack the pages in order with the title page on top.

4. Staple together the pages along the left-hand side.

September, Week 1: First Day of School

(pages 11–12)
Format: standard mini-book
On the last page, invite children to write what they are looking forward to in the new school year.

September, Week 2: All the Way to School

(pages 13–15)
Format: shape book
Cut out the bus-shaped pages and then follow the standard format assembly instructions. On the last page, have children write how they get to school, following the language pattern.

September, Week 3: The Story of ME!

(pages 16–18)
Format: standard mini-book
Each page of the mini-book prompts children to draw and write about themselves. Have children draw themselves on the cover.

September, Week 4: Leaf Walk (pages 19–20)

Format: "pocket" book

1. Begin with the sheet with the title page. Cut apart the mini-book pages along the dotted lines.

2. Position the second sheet horizontally. Cut along the horizontal line to create two long panels. Cut apart mini-book pages 4 and 5.

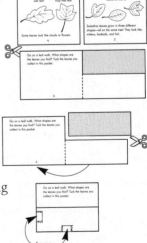

3. On the remaining panel, cut out the shaded box. This will leave a flap.

4. Fold the flap forward along the solid line. Tape the flap on the left side of page 6 to create a pocket.

5. Stack the pages in order with the title page on top and the pocket at the bottom. Staple the pages together along the left edge.

October, Week 1:
The Seasons of an Apple Tree
(pages 21–23)
Format: stand-up book

1. Make **double-sided photocopies** of pages 21–22 so that mini-book page 1 appears directly behind the title page. Cut out the pages.

2. Make **single-sided photocopies** of page 23 (full tree and stand).

3. Paste the copy of page 23 onto thin poster board. Cut out the tree and stand.

4. Stack the pages in order. Place the title page on top, followed by page 2, page 4, and page 6.

5. Place the pages on the top of the full tree and staple everything together **along the top edge**.

6. Cut a slit in the stand and at the bottom of the tree where indicated. Insert the trunk into the stand to make the book stand up.

October, Week 2:
Dinosaur Riddles
(pages 24–25)
Format: standard mini-book

October, Week 3:
Amazing BATS (pages 26–27)
Format: stand-up book

1. Paste the large bat pattern onto poster board or oak tag and cut it out. Color the front and back of the bat, leaving the square in the center blank.

2. Cut apart the mini-book pages along the dotted lines.

3. Stack the mini-book pages in order with the title page on top. Staple the pages together along the left-hand side.

4. Place a few dabs of glue on the blank square between the bat's wings. Glue the mini-book onto this square, pressing firmly.

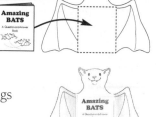

5. Fold each of the bat's wings forward along the dotted lines so that the wings extend over the mini-book in the center. Crease the wings sharply along the folds, then partially open them. Stand the book on a flat surface.

6. On the last page of the book, invite children to write and research their own question about bats.

October, Week 4:
What Should I Be for Halloween?
(pages 28–29)
Format: mixed-up flap book

1. Cut apart the pages of the book along the long dotted lines to create 6 panels. (Do not cut along the short solid lines yet.)

2. Stack the pages in order with the title page on top. Staple the pages together along the left-hand side.

3. Read the book together. Then show children how to open each page and firmly crease it along the centerfold so that the pages of the book lie flat.

4. Cut along the short solid lines on the cover to make three flaps, without cutting all the way to the book's edge. Then cut through pages 2–5 of the book in the same way, creating three flaps on each of these pages. **Do not cut page 6**.

5. Show children how to flip the flaps back and forth to create different mixed-up costumes.

November, Week 1:
Who Hibernates?
(pages 30–31)
Format: standard mini-book

November, Week 2:
My Favorite Color
(pages 32–33)
Format: pop-up book

1. Position the pages horizontally. Cut along the **vertical** dotted lines to create four panels: pages 1–2, pages 3–4, pages 5–6, and the title page/rainbow shape.

2. Cut apart the title page and rainbow shape along the dotted line. Color the rainbow shape and cut it out.

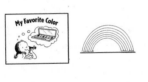

3. Fold the panel with pages 5–6 in half backward along the solid line so that the blank side faces in. Cut the two short tab lines, cutting through both sides of the paper.

4. Unfold the panel, then fold it in half **forward** along the solid line. As you fold, push in the tab. Crease firmly along the fold (including the tab). When you open the panel, a small three-dimensional box will appear.

5. Put a dab of glue on the bottom part of the box. Glue the rainbow to the box. Fold the panel closed again.

6. Fold the panels with pages 1–2 and 3–4 in half forward along the solid line so that the blank sides face out. Stack the folded panels on top of one another so that the mini-book pages are in order and the folded edges are aligned. Place the cover on top. Staple the cover and panels together along the top edge.

7. When you flip through the book, there will be some blank pages. Glue the blank pages together.

November, Week 3:
Take a Trip With a Book
(pages 34–35)
Format: standard mini-book

November, Week 4:
The Pilgrims
(pages 36–37)
Format: standard mini-book

December, Week 1:
What Will the Weather Be?
(pages 38–39)
Format: mixed-up flap book
Follow the directions for "What Should I Be for Halloween?" (October, Week 4).

December, Week 2:
The Mitten Book
(pages 40–41)
Format: shape book
Cut out the mitten-shaped pages and then follow the standard format assembly instructions.

December, Week 3:
Special Days
(pages 42–44)
Format: standard mini-book
Invite children to draw and write about the holiday(s) their families celebrate in December.

December, Week 4: Surprises!

(page 45)

Format: box

1. For added stability, paste the pattern page on heavy paper, such as construction paper. (Note: Folding is more difficult on thick paper. If children are constructing their boxes, provide assistance with folding.)

2. Color the illustrations to resemble wrapping paper. Cut out the pattern along the solid lines.

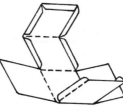

3. Fold backward along all the dotted lines. Fold the pages into a box, with the title at the top and page 5 on the bottom.

4. Tape the sides and bottom of the box together. Do not tape down the top flap. Instead, tuck in the tab to close the box.

5. Invite children to store a poem or small "treasure" inside the box, tie it with a ribbon, and give it as a surprise to someone special.

January, Week 1: A Brand-New Year

(pages 46–48)

Format: standard mini-book
Have children fill in the names of the months on each page.

January, Week 2: A Penguin Year

(pages 49–50)

Format: step book

1. Cut apart the mini-book pages along the dotted lines.

2. Stack the pages in order with the cover on top, followed by winter, spring, summer, and fall.

3. Align the pages along the top edge and staple them together.

January, Week 3: Meet Martin Luther King, Jr.

(pages 51–52)

Format: standard mini-book

January, Week 4: The Dragon Parade

(page 53)

Format: accordion book
Note: The Chinese New Year falls between late January and mid-February.

1. Cut out the page along the dotted lines. Fold the page in half backward along the solid line.

2. Color the dragon.

3. Flip the book over. Fold the pages along the solid lines. To create the accordion effect, re-fold backward along the first line, forward along the second line, and backward along the last line. Firmly crease the pages.

4. Dab a small amount of glue on the top part of a craft stick, on both the front and the back. Insert the craft stick between the front and back panels of the book on one end. Press firmly to glue the stick in place. Repeat with a second craft stick. Invite children to make the dragon dance by moving the craft sticks up and down.

February, Week 1: Say Good-bye to Winter

(pages 54–55)

Format: pop-up book
Follow the directions for "My Favorite Color" (November, Week 2). In this book, a groundhog pops up on the last page.

February, Week 2:
Be Mine, Valentine!
(pages 56–57)
Format: shape book

Cut out the heart-shaped pages and then follow the standard format assembly instructions. This book also doubles as a Valentine card. Invite children to color and decorate their books, fill in the "To" and "From" lines on the cover, and give it to someone special.

February, Week 3:
The Tooth Book
(pages 58–59)
Format: shape book

Cut out the tooth-shaped pages and then follow the standard format assembly instructions. Staple the pages together along the top of the book.

February, Week 4:
How Do You Count to 100?
(pages 60–63)
Format: standard mini-book

March, Week 1:
A Sky Full of Clouds
(pages 64–65)
Format: shape book

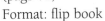

Cut out the cloud-shaped pages and then follow the standard format assembly instructions. Staple the pages together along the left-hand side.

March, Week 2:
The Farmer and the Leprechaun
(pages 66–68)
Format: standard mini-book

March, Week 3:
Hello, Spring!
(pages 69–70)
Format: standard mini-book

March, Week 4:
From Tadpole to Frog
(page 71)
Format: flip book

1. Paste the pattern page onto heavy paper, such as construction paper, covering the entire back of the pattern page with a thin layer of glue.

2. Cut apart the pages along the dotted lines.

3. Stack the pages in order with the title page on top. Make sure to align the pages along the bottom edge.

4. Staple the pages together along the top edge.

5. Show children how to turn the pages of the book slowly to read the text. Then show them how to flip through the pages quickly to watch the tadpole turn into a frog. Hold the top edge of the book with one hand while flipping through the pages using the thumb of the other hand.

April, Week 1:
The Wacky Day
(pages 72–73)
Format: standard mini-book

April, Week 2:
Rain Song
(pages 74–75)
Format: shape book

Cut out the raindrop-shaped pages. Stack the pages in order with the title page on top, punch a hole through the tops of the pages, and bind them together with yarn or string. On the last page, invite children to write the sounds they hear when they listen to the rain.

April, Week 3:
Every Day Is Earth Day
(pages 76–77)
Format: shape book

Cut out the Earth-shaped pages. Stack the pages in order with the title page on top, punch a hole through the tops of the pages, and bind them together with yarn or string. On the last page, invite children to write what they do to take care of our planet.

April, Week 4:
Is It Hard to Grow a Garden?
(pages 78–79)
Format: pop-up book

Follow the directions for "My Favorite Color" (November, Week 2). In this book, flowers pop up on the last page.

May, Week 1:
How Big Is a Whale?
(pages 80–82)
Format: shape book

Cut out the whale-shaped pages and then follow the standard format assembly instructions. Staple the pages together along the left-hand side.

May, Week 2:
I Take Care of My Heart
(pages 83–84)
Format: standard mini-book

On the last page, have children write what they do to keep their hearts healthy.

May, Week 3:
Pet Problem
(pages 85–86)
Format: standard mini-book

May, Week 4:
Becoming a Butterfly
(pages 87–88)
Format: step book
Follow the directions for "A Penguin Year" (January, Week 2).

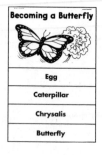

June, Week 1:
Spin, Spider, Spin
(page 89)
Format: flip book
Follow the directions for "From Tadpole to Frog" (March, Week 4).

June, Week 2:
Class Memory Book
(pages 90–92)
Format: standard mini-book

Each page prompts children to write and draw about the highlights of the school year.

June, Week 3:
My Autograph Book
(pages 93–94)
Format: standard mini-book
Have children use the blank

pages inside the book to collect their classmates' autographs. If desired, add blank pages at the end of the book for additional room for autographs.

June, Week 4:
When Summer Comes
(page 95–96)
Format: standard mini-book
On the last page, invite children to write about their summer plans.

First Day of School

I can't wait to meet my teacher.

1

I can't wait to see my friends.

2

I can't wait to use my new notebook, my new pencils, and my new pens.

3

I can't wait for this bus to get there.

4

I can't wait for the bell to ring.

5

I can't wait to begin the adventures
this new school year is sure to bring!

6

What are you looking forward to this new
school year?

_____

_____

_____

7

All the Way to School

(Sing to the tune of "The Wheels on the Bus.")

If I were a snake, I'd slither and slide,
slither and slide, slither and slide.
If I were a snake, I'd slither and slide
all the way to school.

I

If I were a rabbit, I'd hippity-hop,
hippity-hop, hippity-hop.
If I were a rabbit, I'd hippity-hop
all the way to school.

2

If I were a bird, I'd flip-flap-fly,
flip-flap-fly, flip-flap-fly.
If I were a bird, I'd flip-flap-fly
all the way to school.

3

If I were a bug, I'd creep and crawl,
creep and crawl, creep and crawl.
If I were a bug, I'd creep and crawl
all the way to school.

4

But I am a person, so I

_____,

_____,

_____.

But I am a person, so I

_____,

_____,

all the way to school.

5

Write how
you get to
school.

Mini-Book of the Week Scholastic Teaching Resources

The Story of ME!

by _____

I am _____ years old.

My birthday is _____.

There are _____ people in my family and _____ pets.
These are the people in my family:

_____

_____

2

These are some things I like to do for fun:

_____

_____

3

My favorite food is _____.

My favorite animal is _____.

My favorite book is _____.

4

You should get to know me. You will like me because

_____

_____

5

Mini-Book of the Week Scholastic Teaching Resources

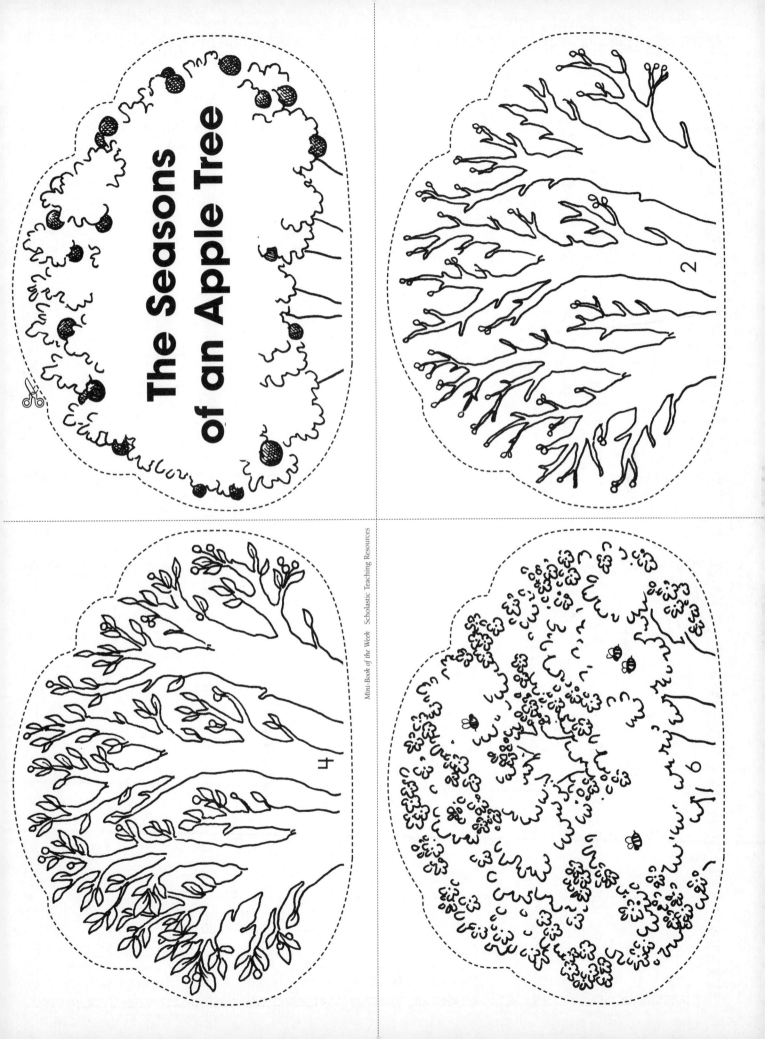

The Seasons of an Apple Tree

2

4

6

Spring

The weather turns warmer. New green leaves uncurl from some buds. Warm sunshine makes the leaves grow.

3

Winter

The weather is cold, and the apple tree seems bare. But look closely and you can see small buds. The tree and buds will rest through the winter.

1

Fall

The flower petals fall from the tree and apples grow. Each apple holds seeds that might become new apple trees.

7

Summer

Now the flower buds burst into bloom. In time, some of the flowers will become apples.

5

Leaf Walk

In autumn, leaves turn colors and fall to the ground. Different trees have leaves that are different sizes and shapes.

1

redbud leaf

gingko leaf

Some leaves look like fans or hearts.

3

willow leaf

sweet gum leaf

Some leaves look like stars or feathers.

2

Mini-Book of the Week Scholastic Teaching Resources

sassafras leaves

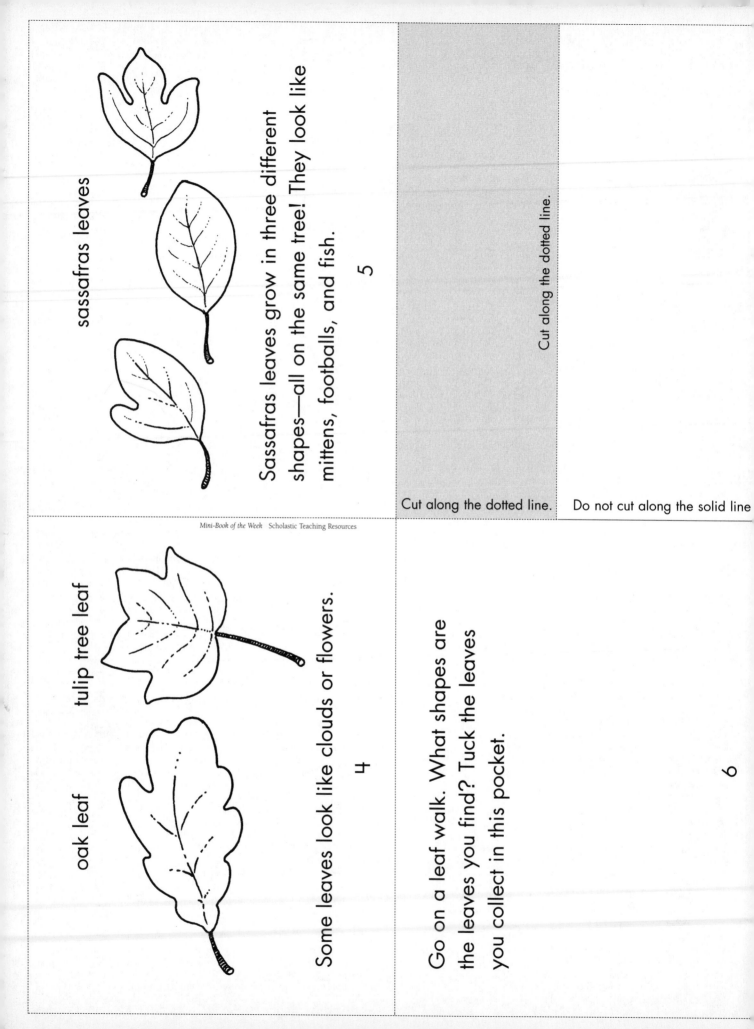

Sassafras leaves grow in three different shapes—all on the same tree! They look like mittens, footballs, and fish.

5

Mini-Book of the Week   Scholastic Teaching Resources

Cut along the dotted line.

Cut along the dotted line.

Cut along the dotted line.

Do not cut along the solid line

oak leaf   tulip tree leaf

Some leaves look like clouds or flowers.

4

Go on a leaf walk. What shapes are the leaves you find? Tuck the leaves you collect in this pocket.

6

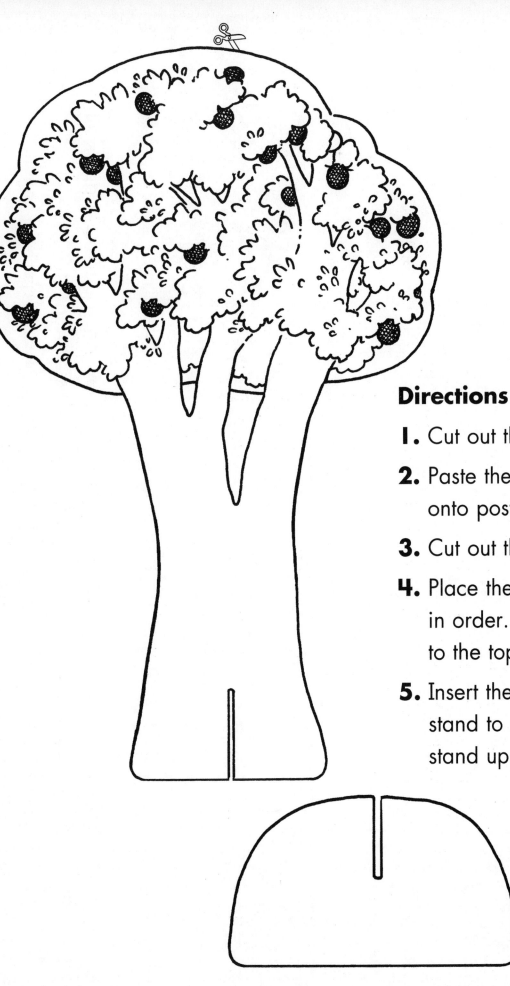

Directions

1. Cut out the book pages.

2. Paste the tree and stand onto poster board.

3. Cut out the tree and stand.

4. Place the book pages in order. Staple them to the top of the tree.

5. Insert the trunk into the stand to make the tree stand up.

Answer: Because they're tons of fun!

Why do dinosaurs get invited to lots of parties?

1

Answer: Tickle its funny bone.

3

How do you make a dinosaur skeleton laugh?

Ha–ha–ha!

Dinosaur Riddles

Mini-Book of the Week   Scholastic Teaching Resources

Answer: A dino-snore.

2

What do you call a dinosaur that sleeps all day?

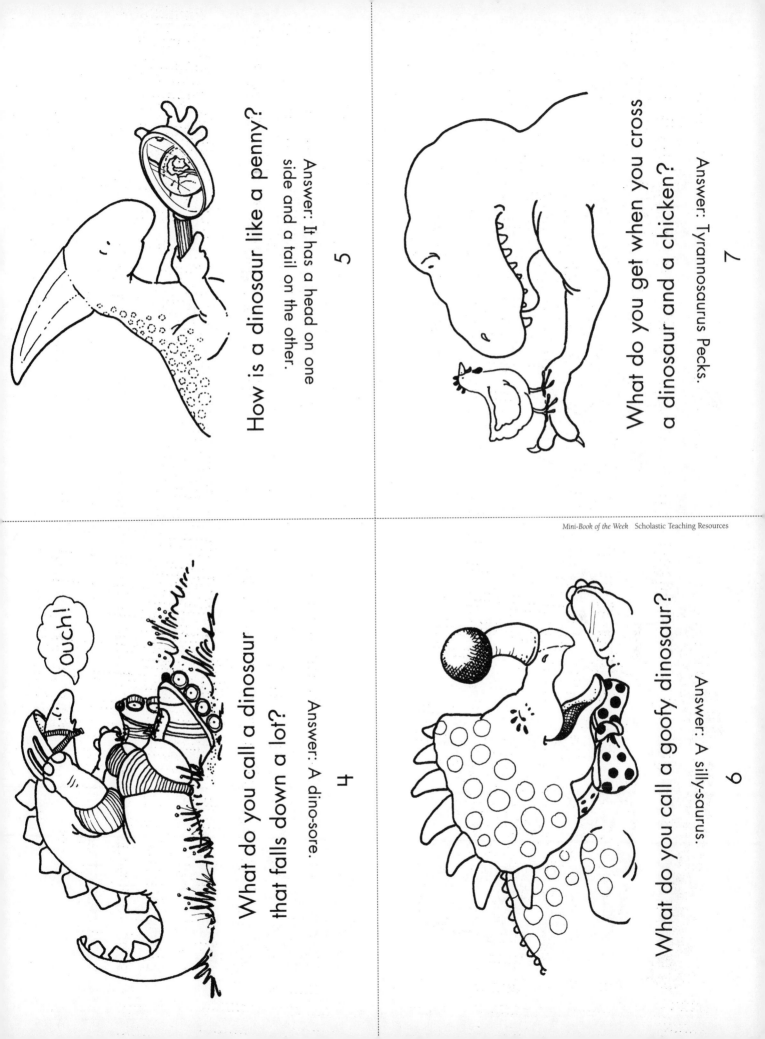

Answer: Tyrannosaurus Pecks.

What do you get when you cross a dinosaur and a chicken?

7

Answer: It has a head on one side and a tail on the other.

How is a dinosaur like a penny?

5

Ouch!

Answer: A dino-sore.

What do you call a dinosaur that falls down a lot?

4

Answer: A silly-saurus.

What do you call a goofy dinosaur?

6

Do bats drink blood?

Only vampire bats drink blood. They feed on the blood of horses and cows, but not people! Most bats eat insects or fruit. A brown bat can eat 150 mosquitoes in 15 minutes!

2

Are bats birds?

No, bats are mammals. They are covered with fur, not feathers. Birds lay eggs, but bats give birth to live young like other mammals. Bats are the only mammal that flies.

1

Amazing BATS

A Question-and-Answer Book

3

Do you have a question about bats? Write it here. Try to find the answer. Write the answer on the blank page opposite this one.

_____

_____

_____

5

Mini-Book of the Week   Scholastic Teaching Resources

How big is a bat?

There are many different kinds of bats, in many different sizes. The smallest bat is the size of a large bumblebee. The biggest bat is the size of a pigeon, with a wingspan of up to six feet.

4

Are bats blind?

No, some bats can see as well as people. But like people, they see better in the daylight than at night. Bats use their powerful sense of hearing to find food at night.

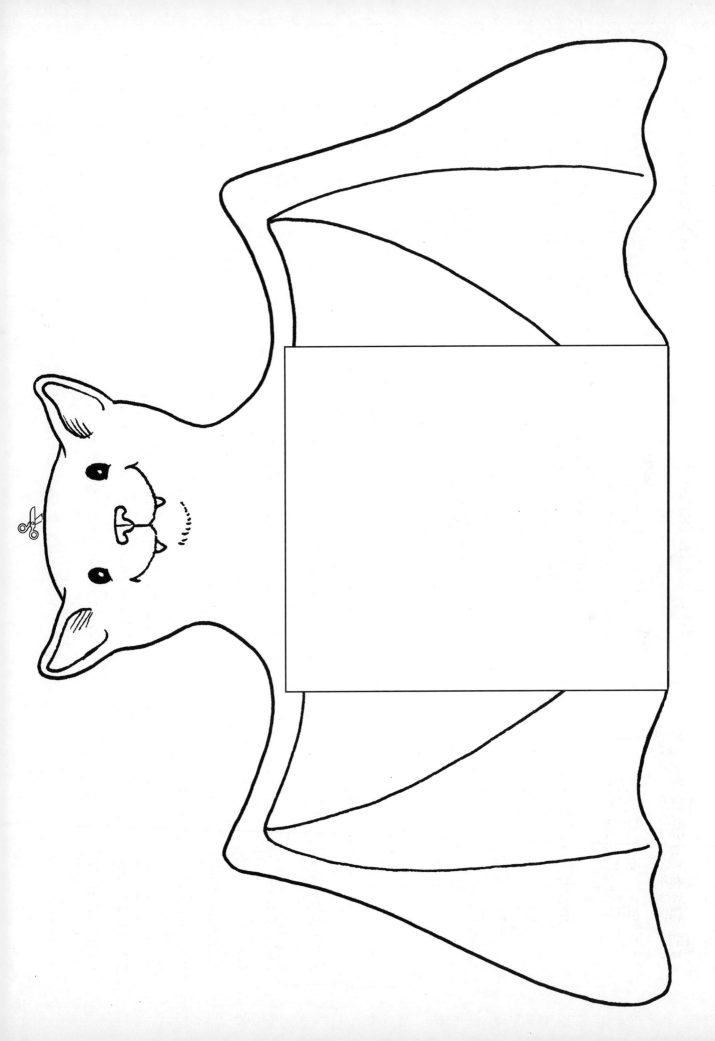

What Should I Be for Halloween?

Maybe I'll be a monster
with a scary face.

Maybe I'll be a skeleton

2

or an alien from space.

3

Cut each page along the solid lines.

Open the flaps back and forth to make silly, mixed-up creatures.

How many different creatures can you make?

Or maybe I'll be a mixed-up creature no one has ever seen before!

6

or a lion that can roar.

5

Maybe I'll be a dragon

4

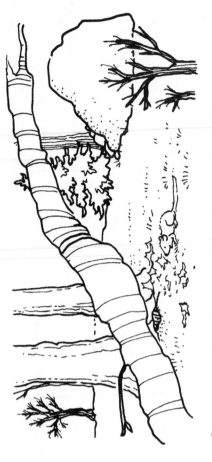

Some animals spend winter in a long, deep sleep. This is called *hibernation*. Who hibernates?

1

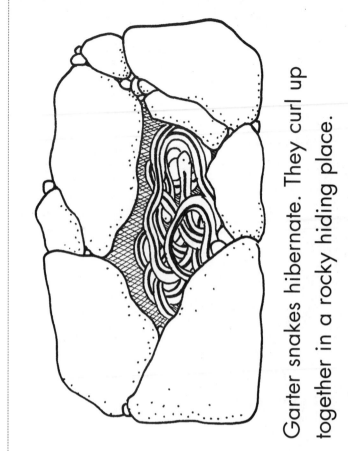

Garter snakes hibernate. They curl up together in a rocky hiding place.

3

Who Hibernates?

Dormice hibernate. They sleep in a cozy underground nest.

2

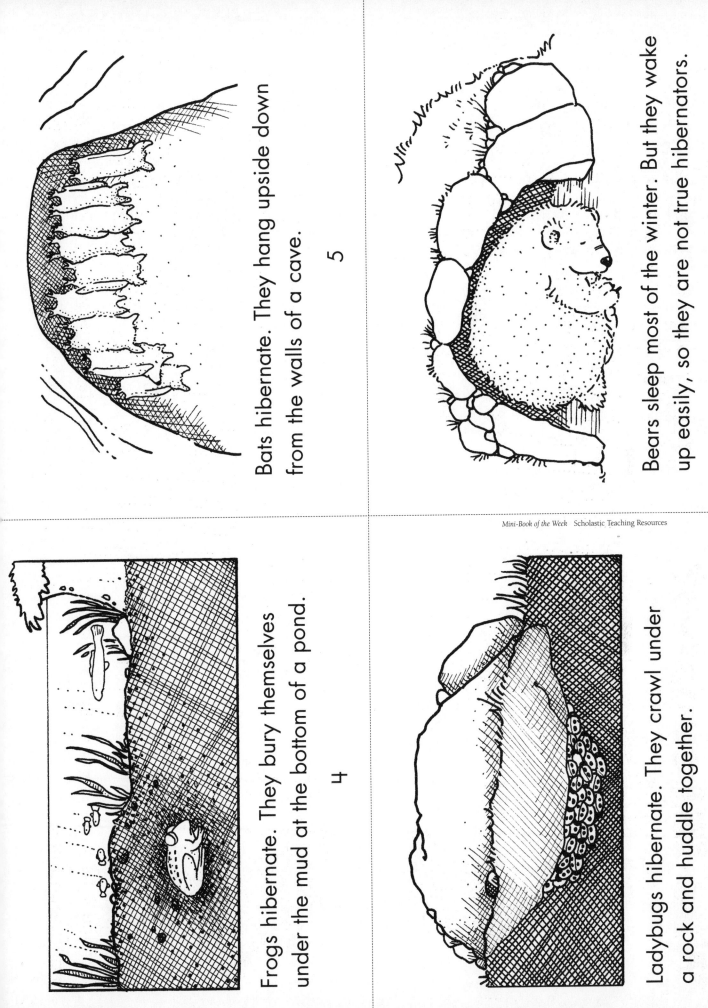

Bats hibernate. They hang upside down from the walls of a cave.

5

Bears sleep most of the winter. But they wake up easily, so they are not true hibernators.

7

Frogs hibernate. They bury themselves under the mud at the bottom of a pond.

4

Ladybugs hibernate. They crawl under a rock and huddle together.

6

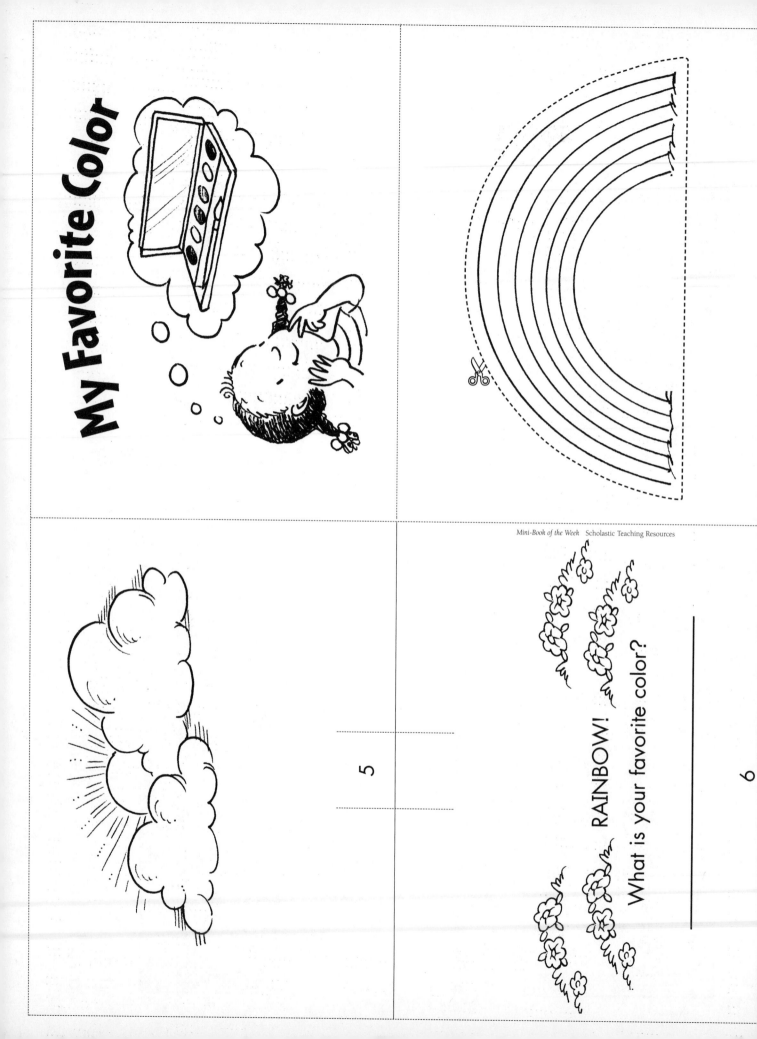

My Favorite Color

5

RAINBOW!

What is your favorite color?

_____

6

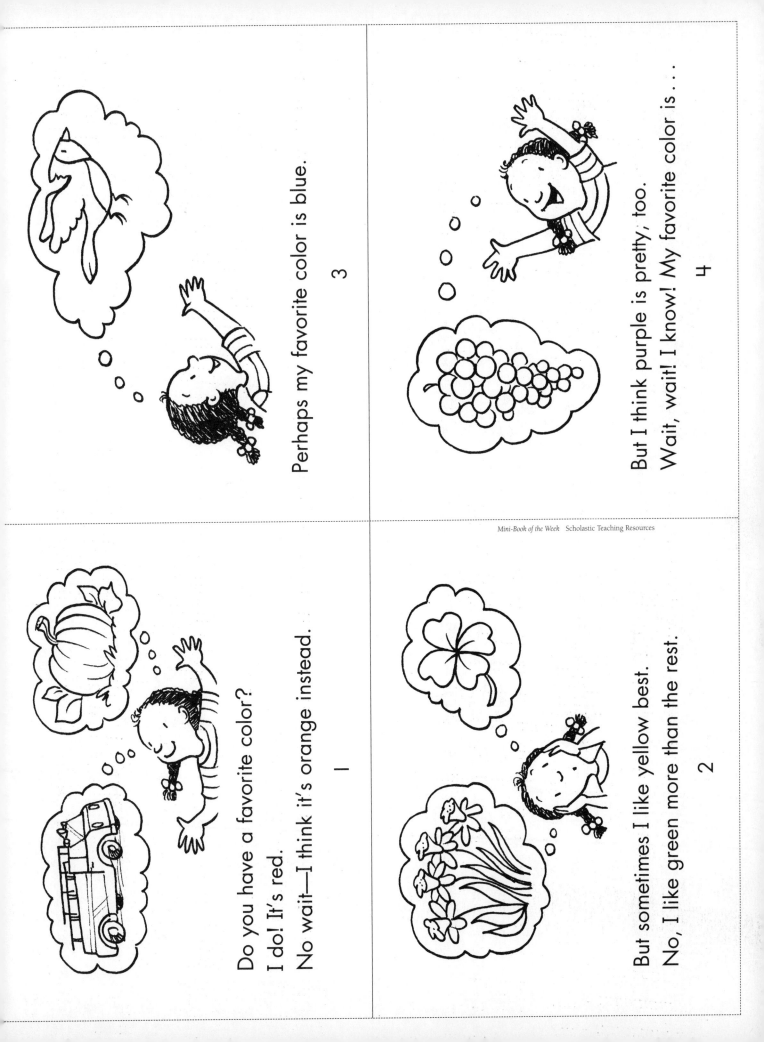

Perhaps my favorite color is blue.

3

But I think purple is pretty, too.
Wait, wait! I know! My favorite color is....

4

Mini-Book of the Week   Scholastic Teaching Resources

Do you have a favorite color?
I do! It's red.
No wait—I think it's orange instead.

1

But sometimes I like yellow best.
No, I like green more than the rest.

2

Take a Trip With a Book

Would you like to see amazing things,

1

explore outer space,

3

visit castles, queens, and kings,

2

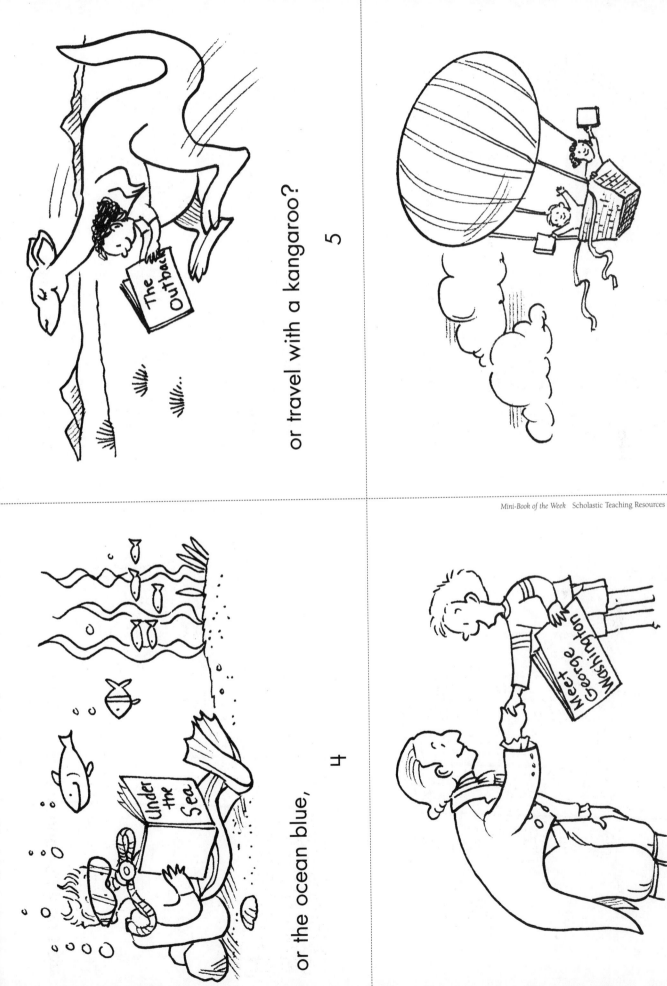

or the ocean blue,

4

or travel with a kangaroo?

5

Are there people you would like to know?

6

Just open up a book and GO!

7

The Pilgrims

In 1620, the Pilgrims left their home in England. They wanted to begin a new life in a new land.

1

The Pilgrims landed near Plymouth Bay in Massachusetts. They built a new town there.

3

They sailed a ship called the *Mayflower* across a stormy sea.

2

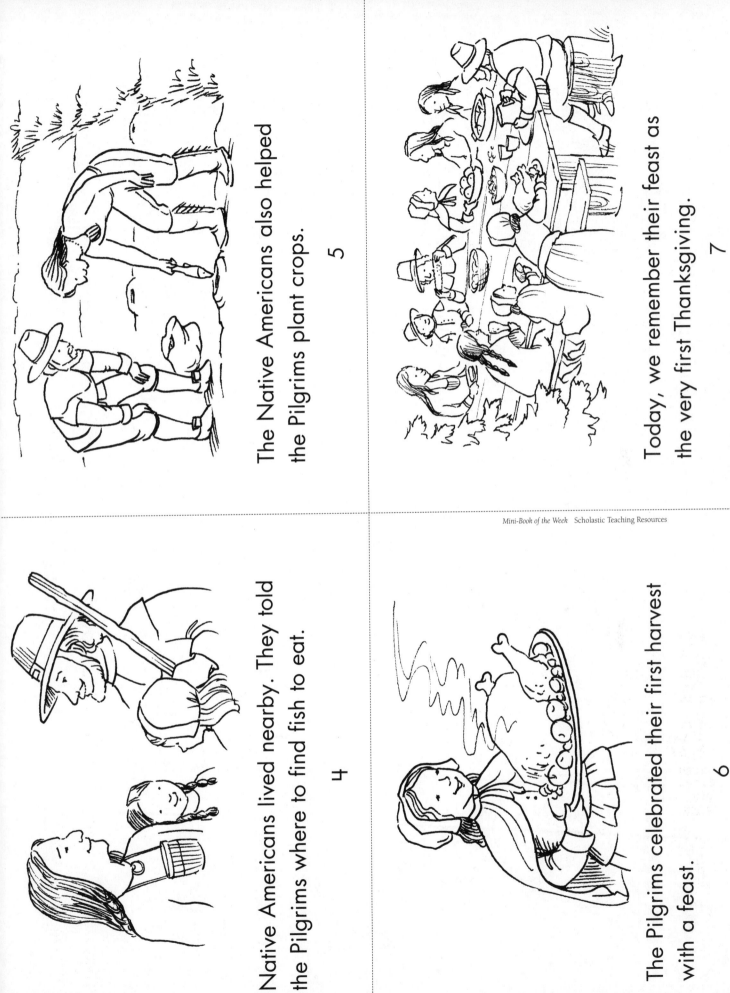

Native Americans lived nearby. They told the Pilgrims where to find fish to eat.

4

The Native Americans also helped the Pilgrims plant crops.

5

The Pilgrims celebrated their first harvest with a feast.

6

Today, we remember their feast as the very first Thanksgiving.

7

What Will the Weather Be?

Will there be ice?

Will there be snow?

2

Will there be winds that blow and blow?

3

Cut each page along the solid lines.

Flip the flaps back and forth to make mixed-up outfits.

How many silly outfits can you create?

Whatever the weather,
I'm ready for fun!

6

Will there be sun?

5

Will there be rain?

4

The Mitten Book

Mittens are just right
for keeping hands
warm and dry,

1

for catching snowflakes
that fall from the sky,

2

for making pretty
snow angel wings,

3

for building snow forts,

4

for pulling things,

5

for making snowballs
and jolly snowmen.

6

Hooray for mittens—
your hands' best friends!

7

Special Days

by _____

Lots of families celebrate special days in December.

My family celebrates _____.

1

Some of the things we do during this holiday are

_____

_____

2

Some of the foods we eat are _____

_____

_____

3

This holiday is important because _____

_____

_____

4

The thing I like best about this holiday is _____

_____

_____

5

tape

Is it a treat or
a toy to enjoy?
I like to guess.
It's fun not to know!

3

wrapped up in
paper and tied
with a bow.

2

tape

tape

Surprises!

I like surprises
in all shapes
and sizes,

1

and I like to give
them away!

5

tape

Surprises!
Surprises!
Hip-hip-hooray!
I like to get them…

4

tape

tape

A Brand-New Year

The calendar says January.

A new year has begun—

twelve new months to celebrate,

twelve new months of fun!

1

After January comes _____,

with its Valentine's Day hearts.

2

Then comes windy _____,

when kites fly high and springtime starts.

3

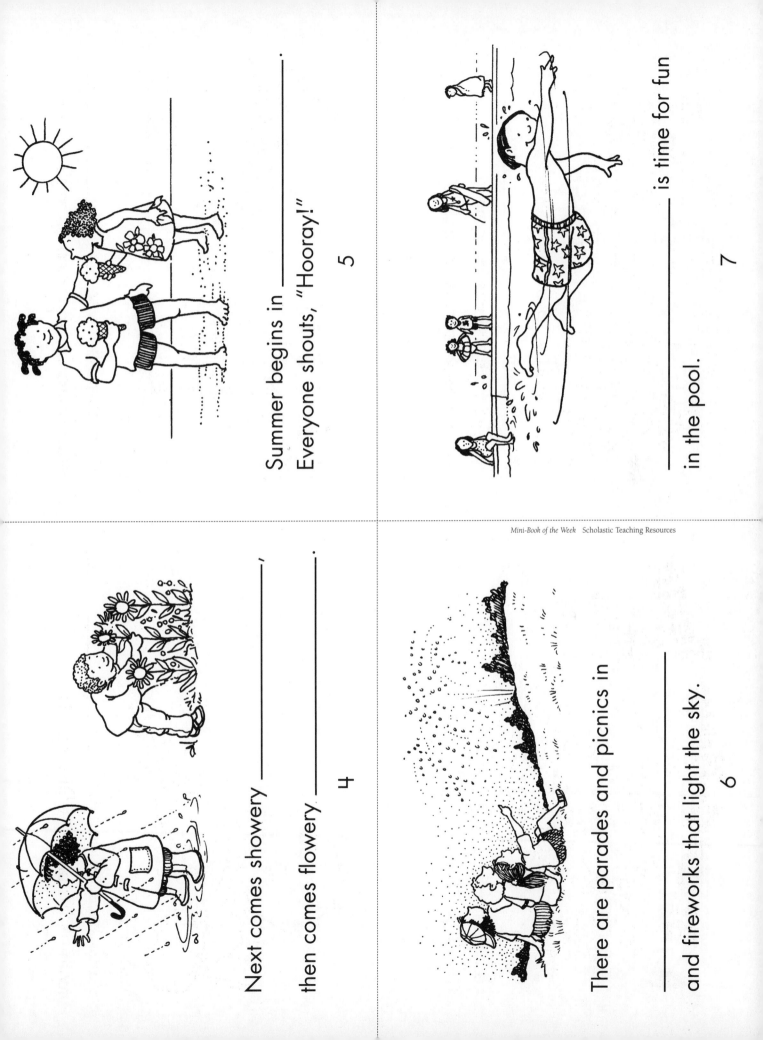

Summer begins in ____.
Everyone shouts, "Hooray!"

5

____ is time for fun

in the pool.

7

Next comes showery ____,

then comes flowery ____.

4

There are parades and picnics in ____

and fireworks that light the sky.

6

In _____

it's time for tricks and treats,

when ghosts and goblins fill the streets.

9

Fall starts in _____.

Time for school!

8

Winter begins in _____,

with lots of special days to remember.

At last, another year is done.

Are you ready for another one?

11

_____ comes,

it's time once more

to think of all we're thankful for.

10

A Penguin Year

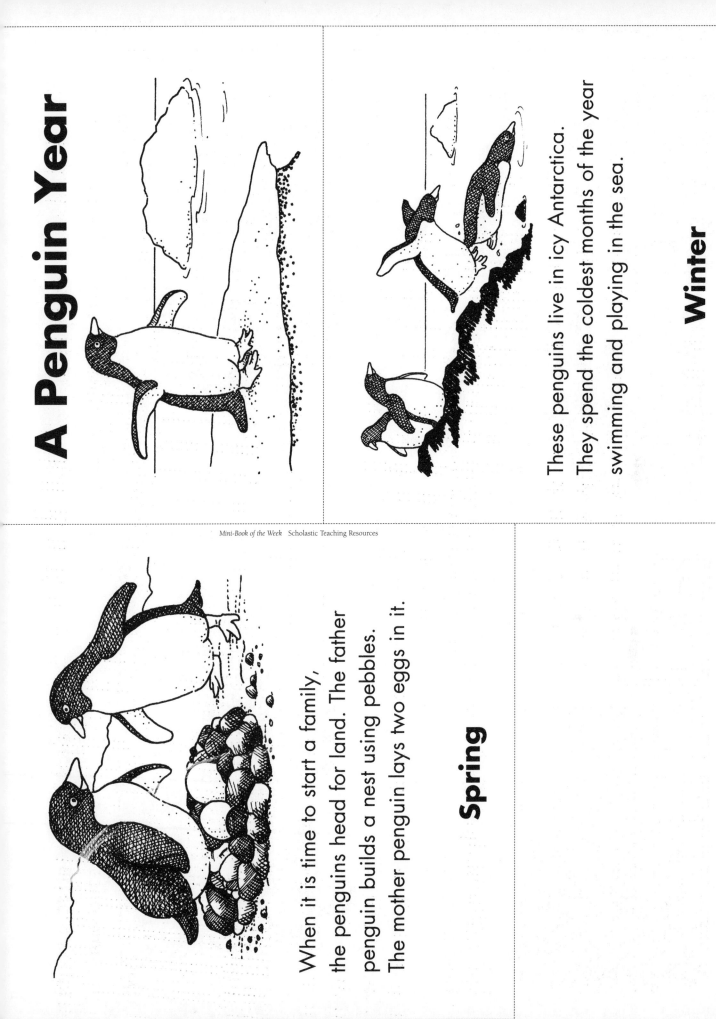

These penguins live in icy Antarctica.
They spend the coldest months of the year
swimming and playing in the sea.

Winter

When it is time to start a family,
the penguins head for land. The father
penguin builds a nest using pebbles.
The mother penguin lays two eggs in it.

Spring

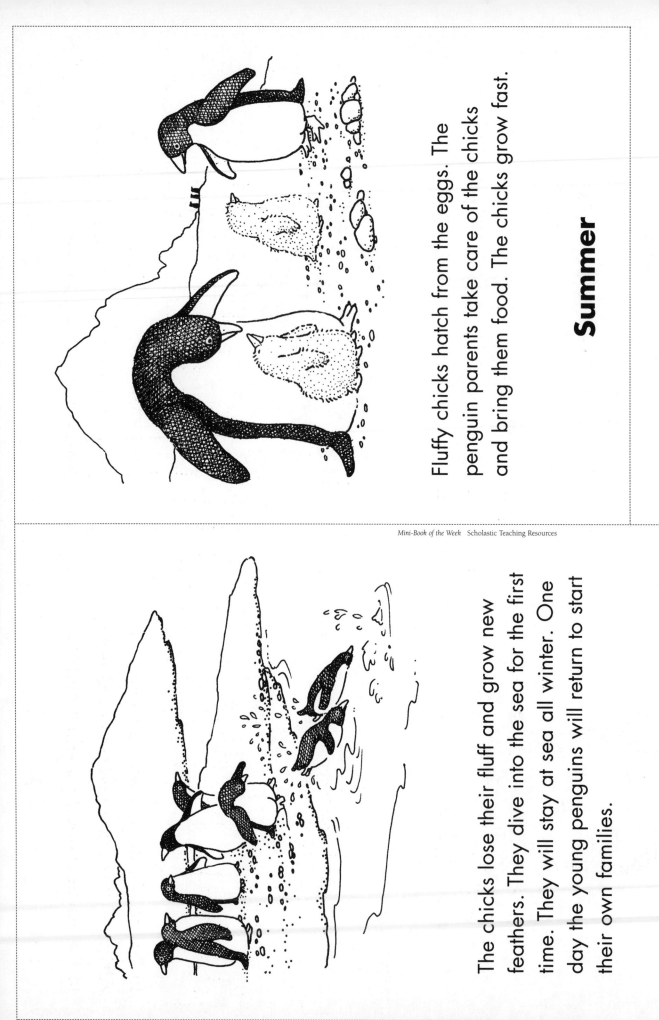

Fluffy chicks hatch from the eggs. The penguin parents take care of the chicks and bring them food. The chicks grow fast.

Summer

The chicks lose their fluff and grow new feathers. They dive into the sea for the first time. They will stay at sea all winter. One day the young penguins will return to start their own families.

Fall

Meet Martin Luther King, Jr.

Dr. Martin Luther King, Jr., was born on January 15, 1929. He lived during a troubling time in our nation's history.

1

In the South, there were laws that said African-American children could not go to the same schools as white children.

2

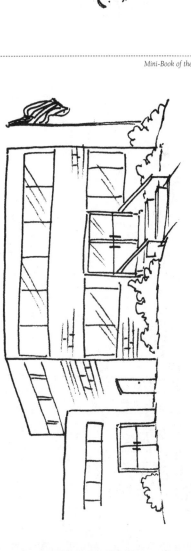

African Americans could not sit near white Americans on buses, in movie theaters, or at restaurants.

3

He talked about his dream for America.

He said he dreamed of a nation where all people could live together as equals.

5

Sadly, Dr. King was killed in 1968. Every January, we celebrate his life and his dream for our nation.

7

EQUAL RIGHTS NOW

Dr. King led marches and gave speeches to try to change the laws.

4

Many people believed in Dr. King's dream. The unfair laws started to change.

6

It will bring
good fortune, too.
Gung Hay Fat Choy!
Happy New Year
to you!

3

Watch it shake
its scales of gold
to chase away
a year that's old.

2

Down the street
the dragon comes,
dancing to the
sound of drums.

1

The
Dragon
Parade

Say Good-bye to Winter

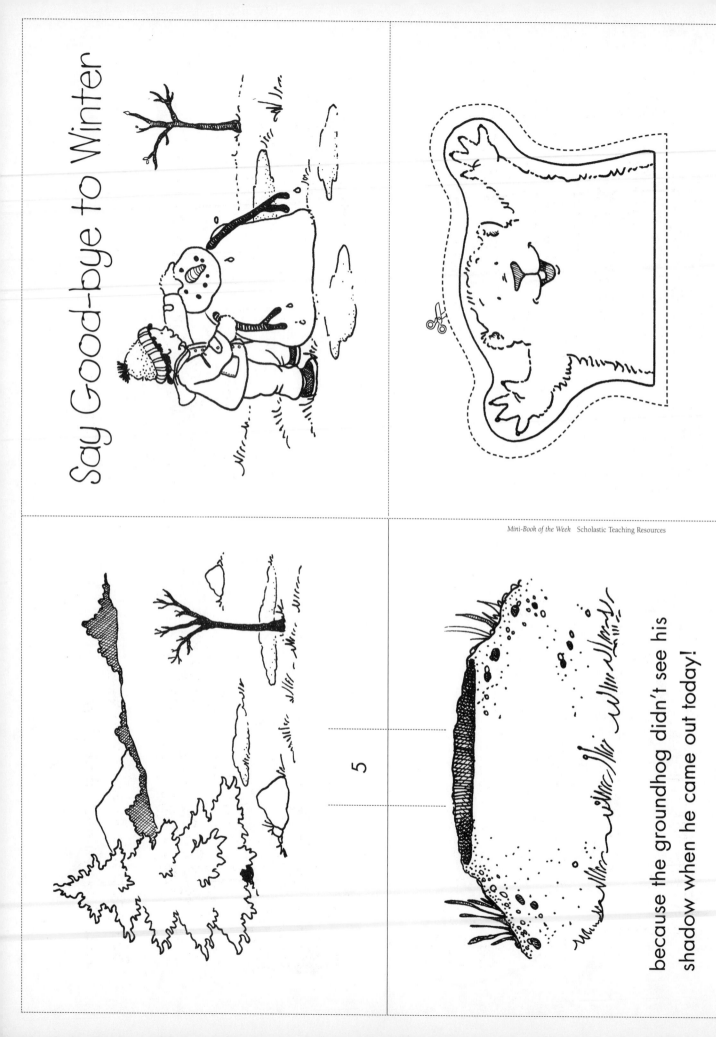

5

because the groundhog didn't see his shadow when he came out today!

6

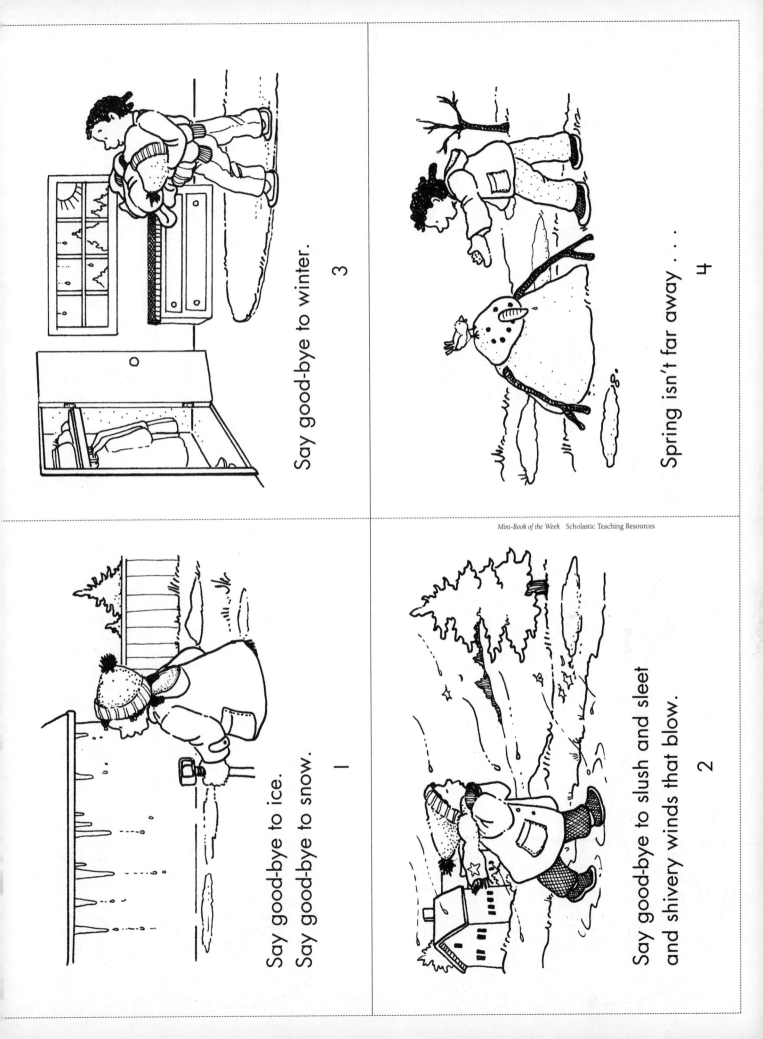

Say good-bye to winter.

3

Spring isn't far away . . . .

4

Say good-bye to ice.
Say good-bye to snow.

1

Say good-bye to slush and sleet
and shivery winds that blow.

2

Flowers love sunshine.

1

Cookies love milk.

3

Be Mine, Valentine!

To: _____

From: _____

Mice love cheese.

2

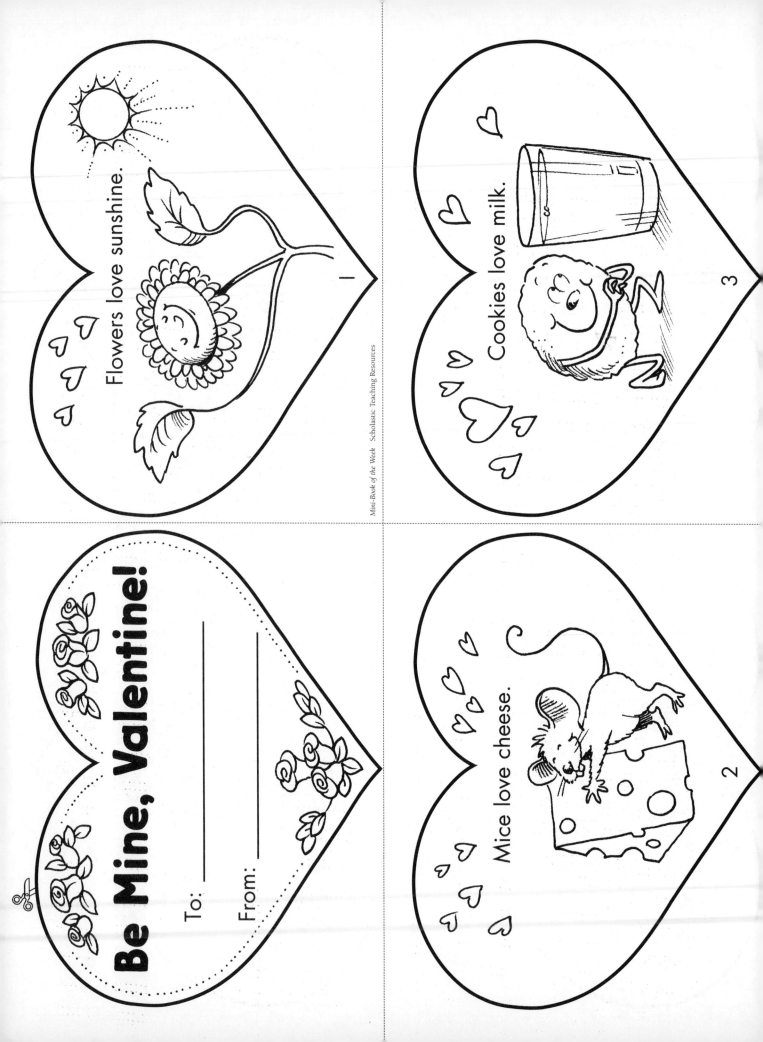

Bees love honey.

5

But not as much as
I LOVE YOU!

7

Apples love trees.

4

A sock loves a shoe.

6

The Tooth Book

Take care of your teeth.
Keep them clean and bright.

1

Brush them every morning.

2

Brush them every night.

3

Choose healthy foods to eat like yogurt, milk, and cheese.

4

Crunchy carrots and apples— teeth like foods like these.

5

See the dentist twice a year to help keep cavities away.

6

Take care of your teeth every single day!

7

How Do You Count to 100?

There are lots of ways to count to 100.
You can count by 1's.

100 lunching, munching ants

1

You can count by 2's.

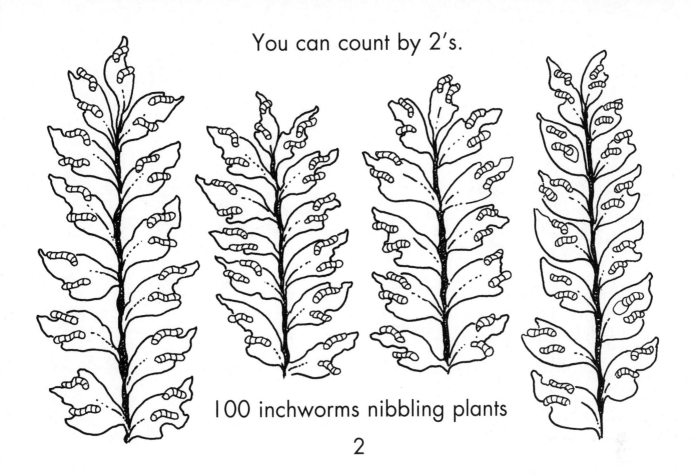

100 inchworms nibbling plants

2

You can count by 5's.

100 spots on ladybugs

3

You can count by 10's.

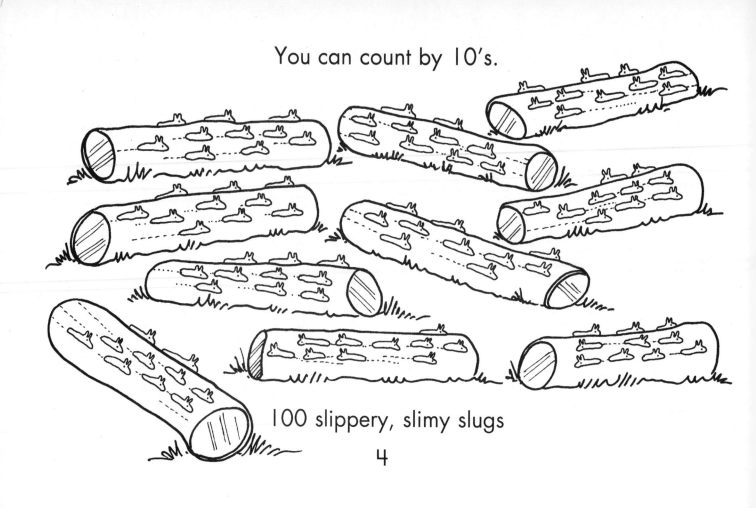

100 slippery, slimy slugs

4

You can count by 20's.

100 busy, buzzy bees

5

You can count by 25's.

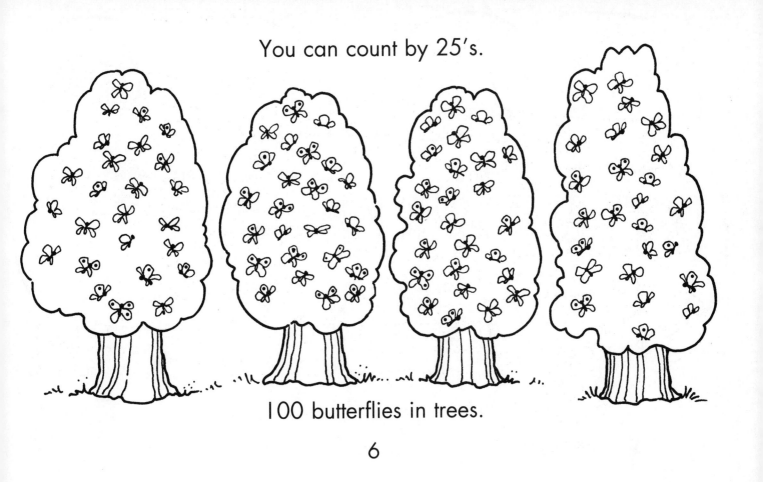

100 butterflies in trees.

You can count by 50's.

100 legs on a centipede
give this creepy-crawly speed.

No matter how you get the job done,
counting to 100 is fun!

A Sky Full of Clouds

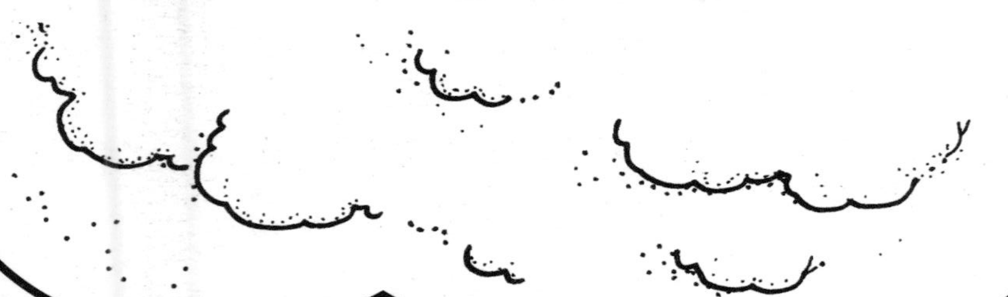

Look up in the sky!
I see a car racing by.

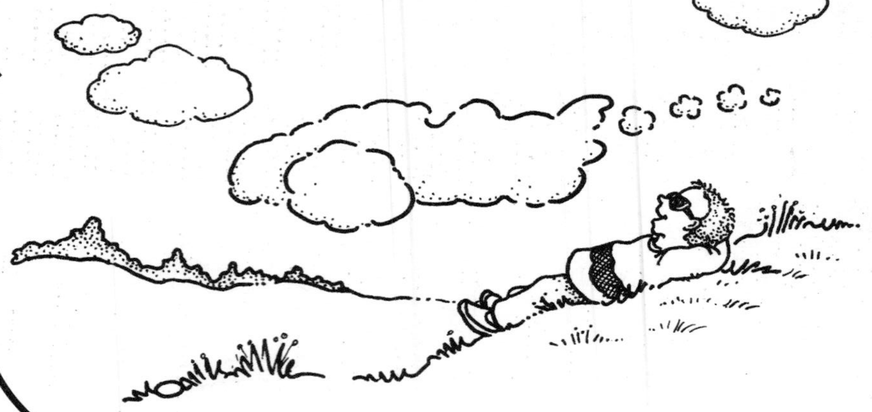

Mini-Book of the Week Scholastic Teaching Resources

I see a hat
and a pair of mittens.

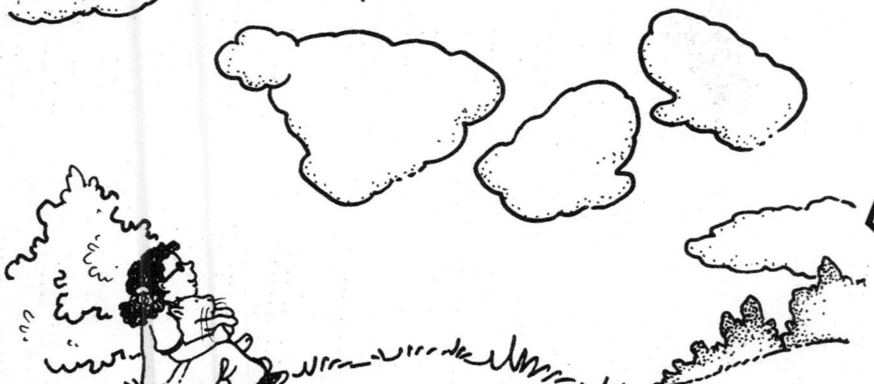

I see a cat
and two little kittens.

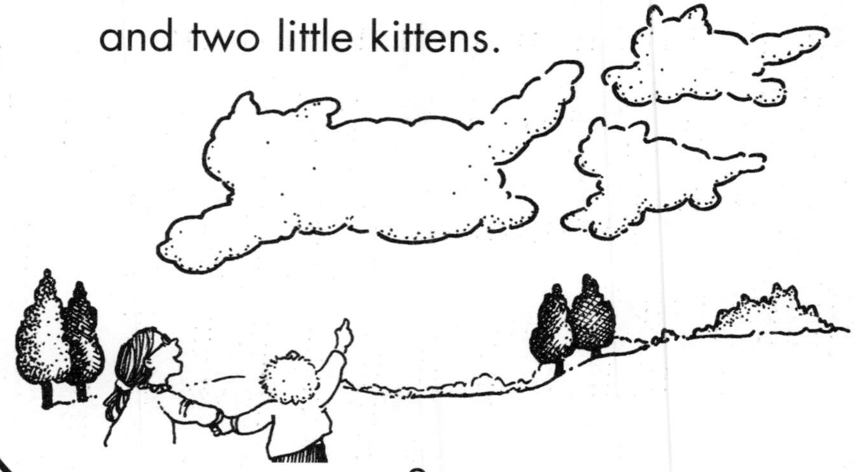

I see some fish
and a great big whale.

5

What do the clouds
look like to you?

7

I see an alligator
with a long bumpy tail.

4

I see a ship sailing
on a sea of blue.

6

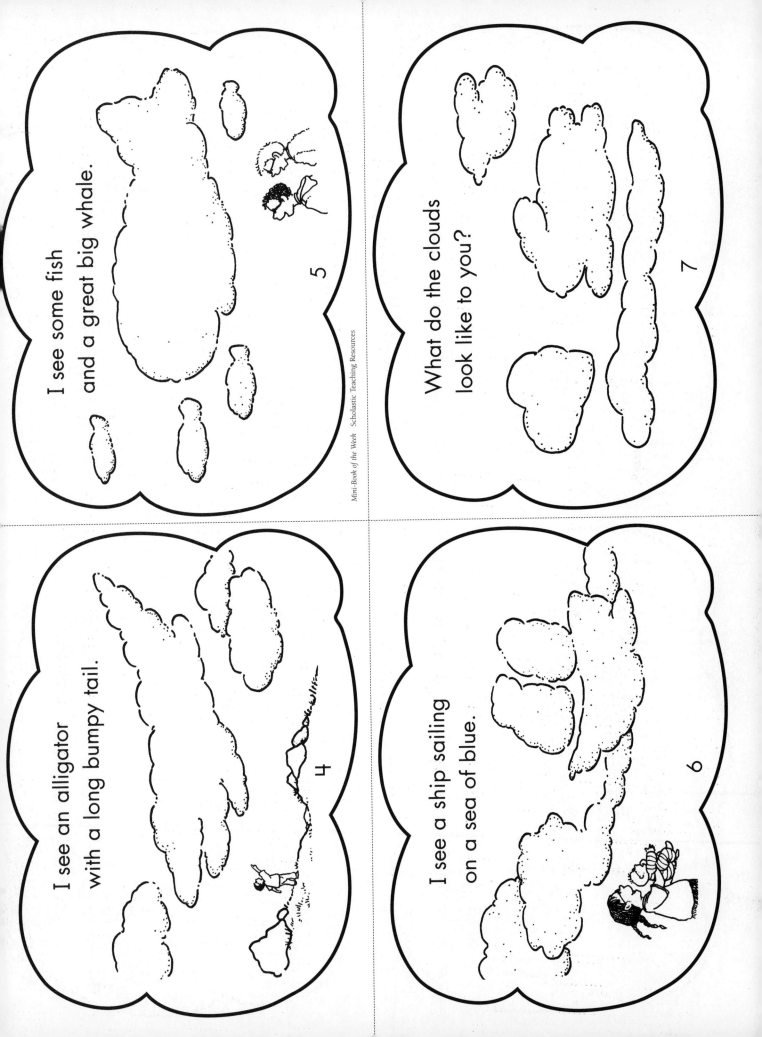

Late one night, a farmer was walking home across a bog. "Help! Help! I'm stuck," he heard a tiny voice cry.

1

"Today is my lucky day!" said the farmer, dancing with joy. "Tell me where your gold is buried, and I will help you."

3

The Farmer and the Leprechaun

A Fairy Tale From Ireland

The farmer saw a wee man caught on a thorn bush. It was a leprechaun!

2

"I'll run home at once and get a shovel," the farmer said. But how would he find the bush again? There were thousands of them in the bog.

5

"It is under this very bush," the leprechaun said. "Now, please, get me down."
The farmer carefully unhooked the tiny man from the thorn.

4

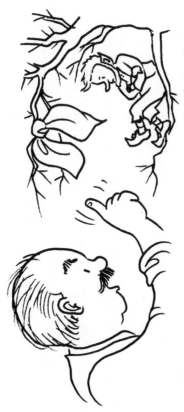

"Promise not to touch that handkerchief, or I'll stick you back on the thorn," said the farmer.
"I promise," said the leprechaun.

7

Then the farmer had an idea. He pulled a bright red handkerchief from his pocket and tied it around the thorn bush.

6

When he returned, the farmer couldn't believe his eyes. The leprechaun had tied a red handkerchief on every thorn bush in the bog!

9

The farmer shook his head and started home again. He knew he wasn't the first person to be tricked by a leprechaun. And he wouldn't be the last.

11

Mini-Book of the Week   Scholastic Teaching Resources

The farmer knew that according to fairy laws, the leprechaun would have to keep his word. So he ran home to get his shovel.

8

The farmer could spend his whole life digging and never find the gold. The leprechaun had outsmarted him!

10

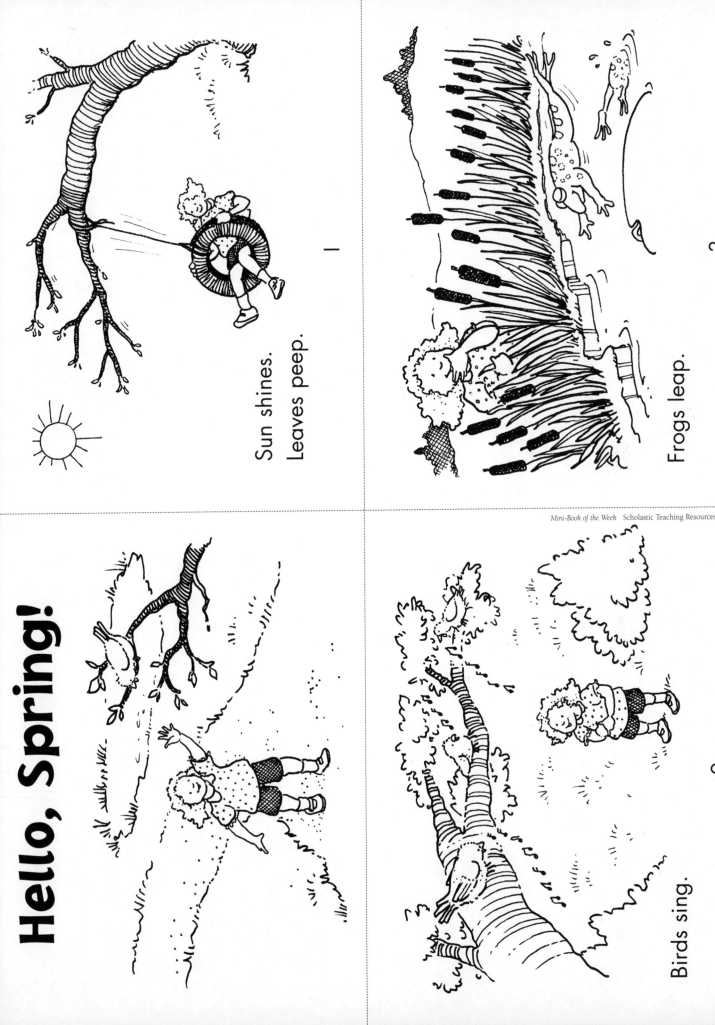

Hello, Spring!

Sun shines.
Leaves peep.

1

Birds sing.

2

Frogs leap.

3

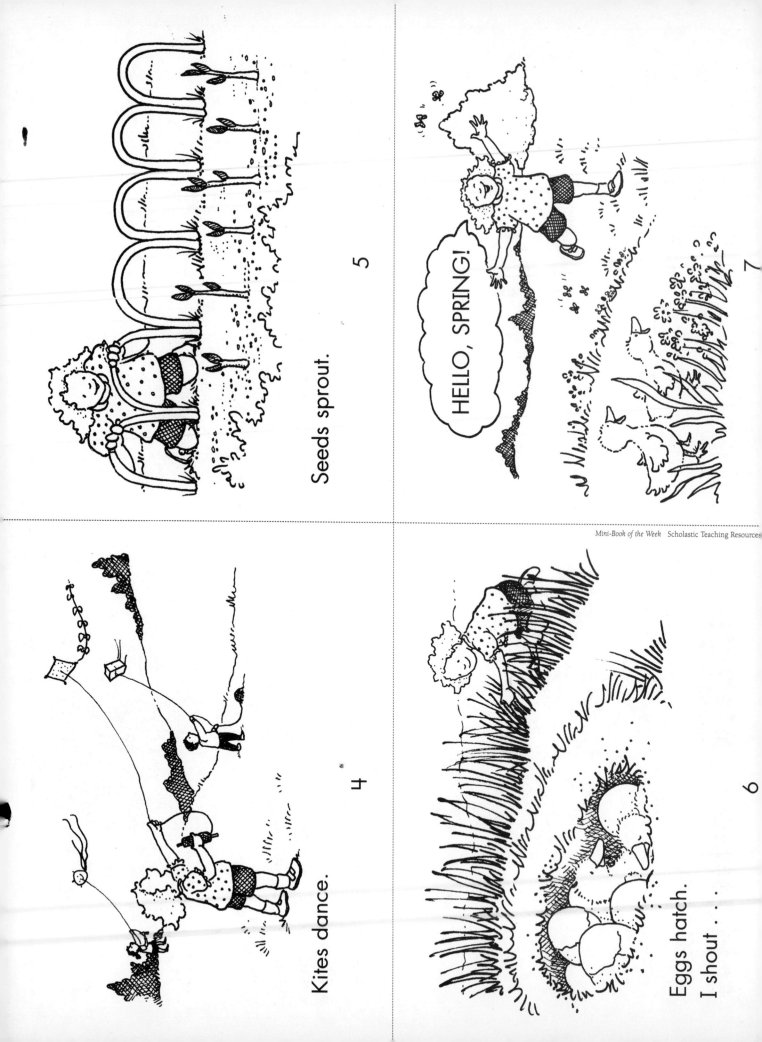

Seeds sprout.

5

HELLO, SPRING!

7

Kites dance.

4

Eggs hatch.
I shout . . .

6

The gills begin to disappear. Back legs begin to grow.

3

The tadpole has feathery gills for breathing underwater.

2

A tiny tadpole hatches from an egg.

1

From Tadpole to Frog

The tadpole has become a frog! Now it will leave the water to live on land.

7

... and shrinks some more. The eyes and mouth grow bigger.

6

The tail shrinks ...

5

Mini-Book of the Week Scholastic Teaching Resources

Front legs begin to grow. Inside, the tadpole is growing lungs for breathing on land.

4

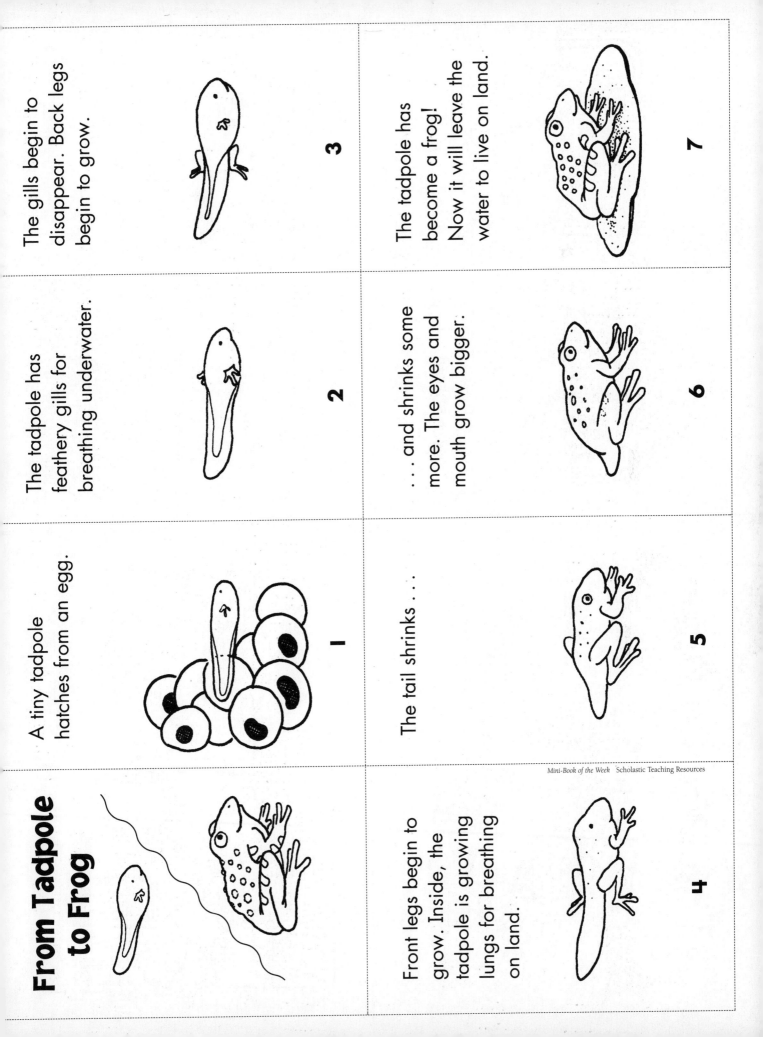

The Wacky Day

You'll never believe what happened today.
Our books grew legs and ran away!

1

Abe Lincoln dropped by for some tea.

3

Spelling Bee Today

gerbil
g-e-r-b-i-l
gerbil

Our gerbil won the spelling bee.

2

The bus flew me home, just like a plane.

5

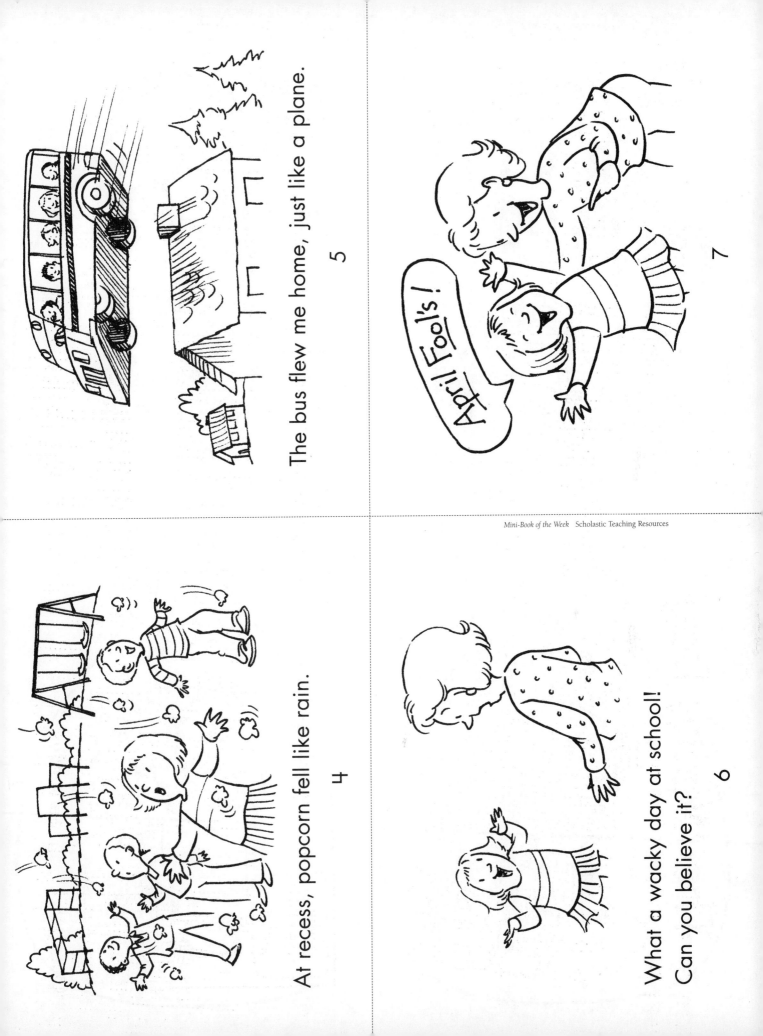

April Fool's!

7

At recess, popcorn fell like rain.

4

What a wacky day at school!
Can you believe it?

6

Rain Song

Rain makes music all day long.
Listen to its noisy song.

1

Tippy, tappy,
drip, drip, drop.

2

Pitter, patter.

3

Splish, splash, plop.

4

Plinka, plinka,
ping, ping, ping.

5

I love the song
that raindrops sing.

6

What does
the rain sound like
to you?

7

Every Day Is Earth Day

Every day is Earth Day.
Every day is a day to care.

1

Every day is a day
to protect our land,

2

protect our water,

3

Is It Hard to Grow a Garden?

5

... you'll have lots of pretty flowers in a row!

6

Mini-Book of the Week   Scholastic Teaching Resources

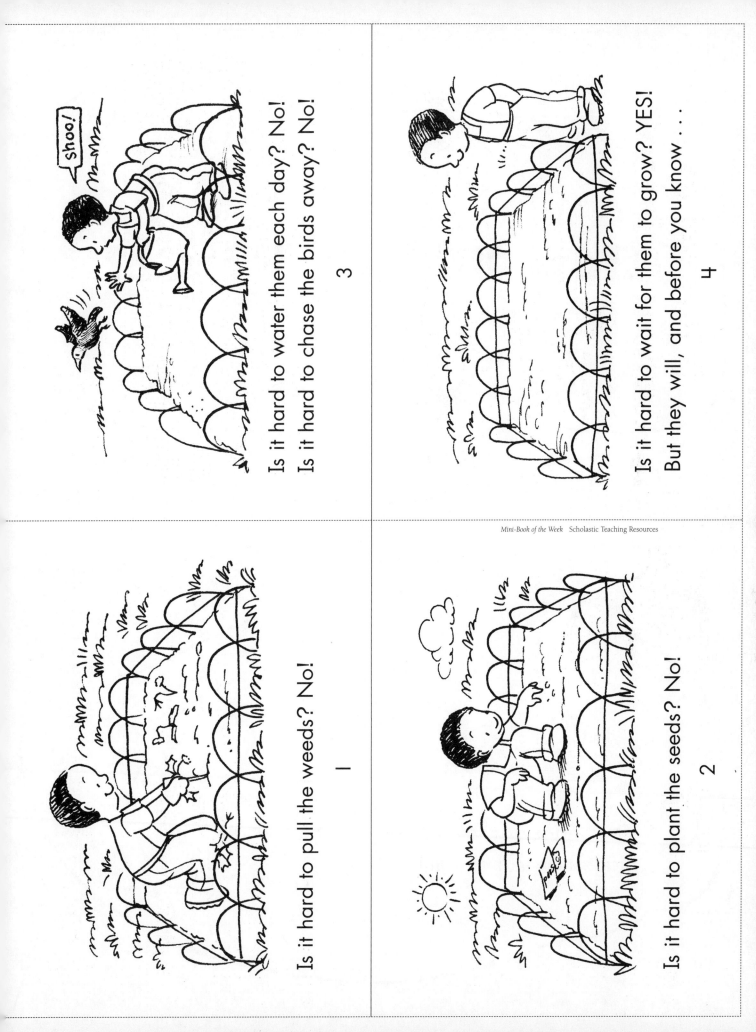

shoo!

Is it hard to water them each day? No!
Is it hard to chase the birds away? No!

3

Is it hard to wait for them to grow? YES!
But they will, and before you know . . .

4

Is it hard to pull the weeds? No!

1

Is it hard to plant the seeds? No!

2

How Big Is a Whale?

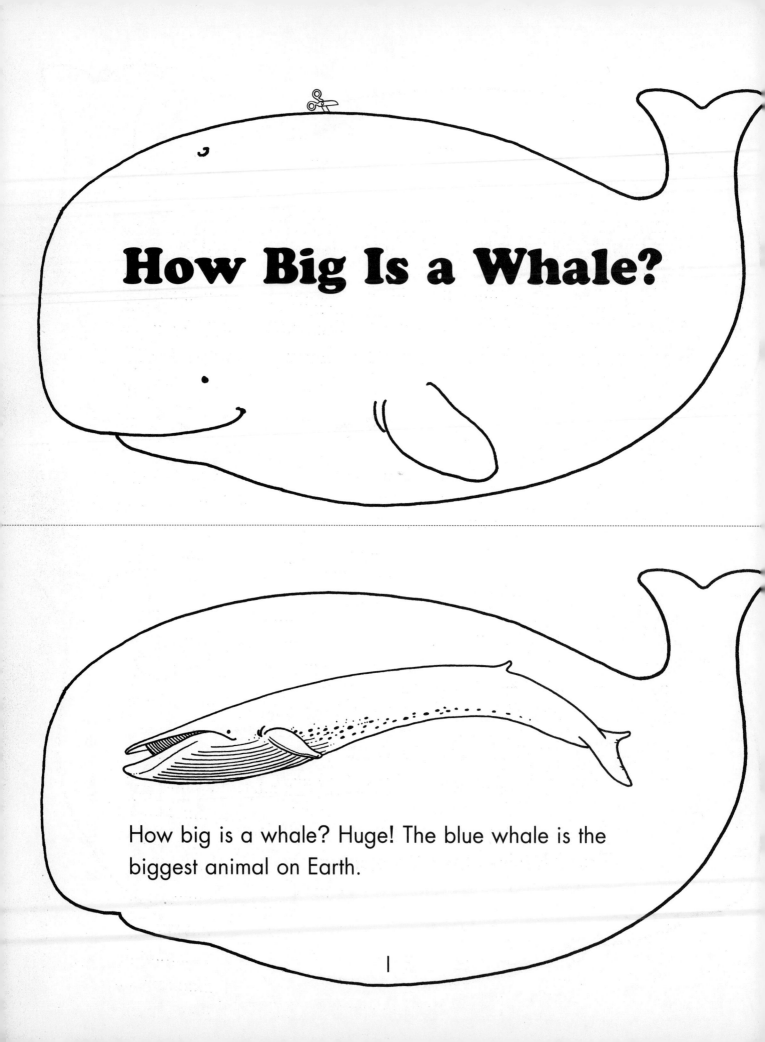

How big is a whale? Huge! The blue whale is the biggest animal on Earth.

1

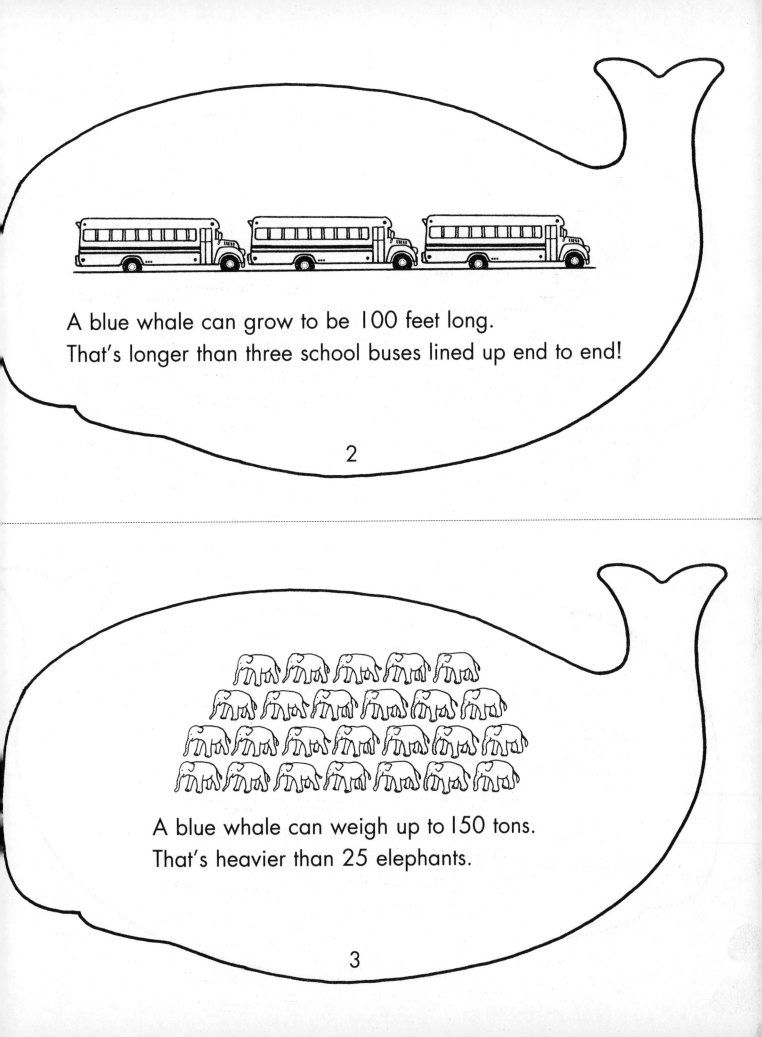

A blue whale can grow to be 100 feet long.
That's longer than three school buses lined up end to end!

2

A blue whale can weigh up to 150 tons.
That's heavier than 25 elephants.

3

Fifty people could stand on the tongue of a blue whale.

4

Scientists think the blue whale is even bigger than most dinosaurs were. Now that's big!

5

I Take Care of My Heart

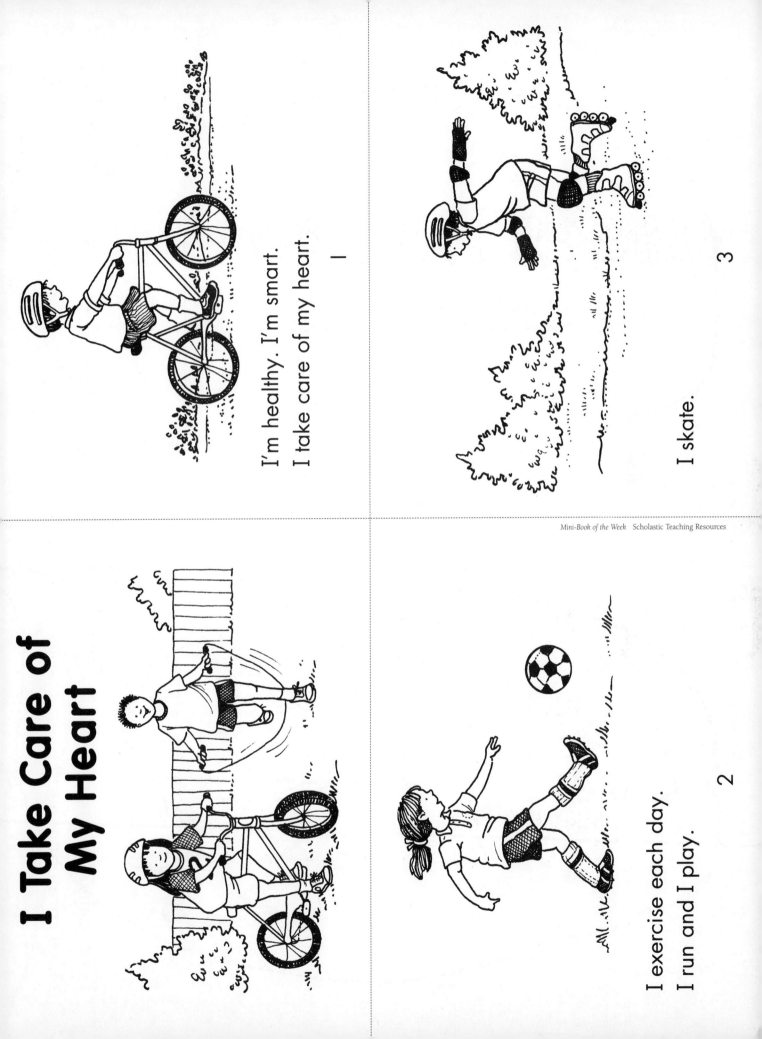

I'm healthy. I'm smart.
I take care of my heart.

1

I exercise each day.
I run and I play.

2

I skate.

3

Mini-Book of the Week   Scholastic Teaching Resources

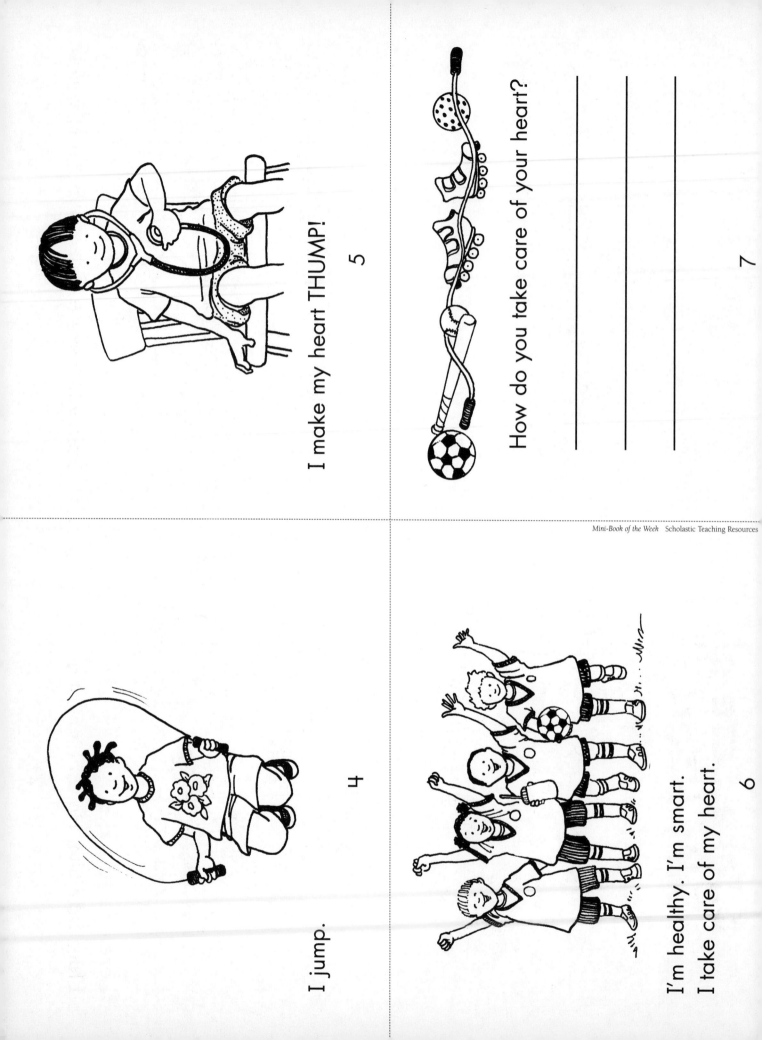

I make my heart THUMP!

5

How do you take care of your heart?

_____

_____

_____

7

I jump.

4

I'm healthy. I'm smart.
I take care of my heart.

6

Pet Problem

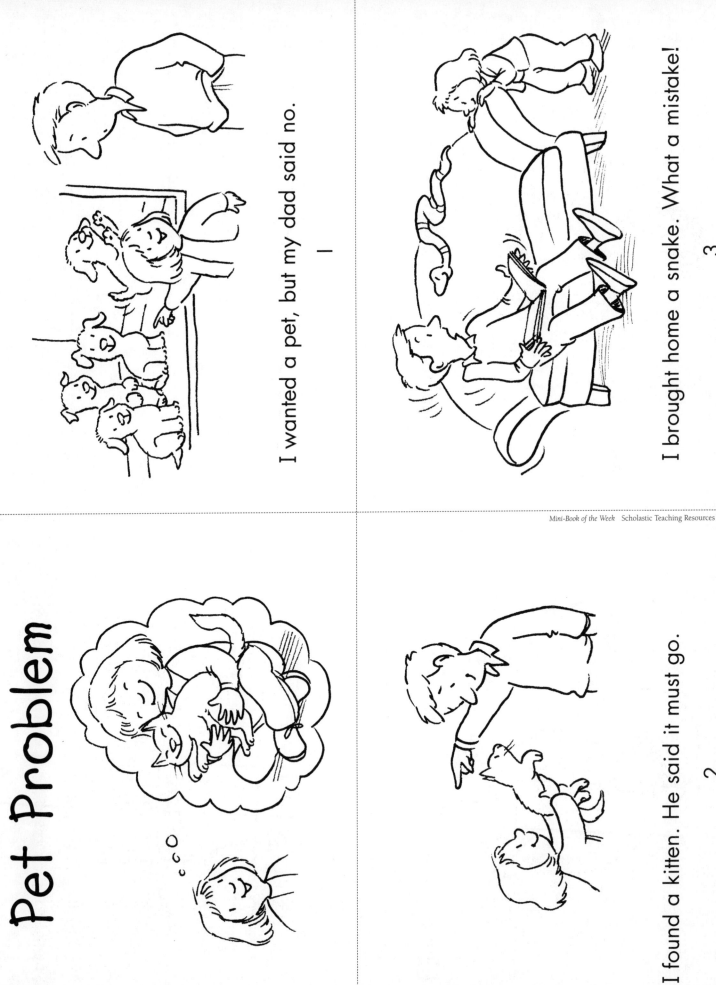

I wanted a pet, but my dad said no.

1

I brought home a snake. What a mistake!

3

I found a kitten. He said it must go.

2

How about a frog or a rabbit instead?
No luck. My dad shook his head.

5

Meet Goldie, my new pet fish!

7

Maybe a mouse? Not in this house!

4

Then finally, one day, I got my wish.

6

Becoming a Butterfly

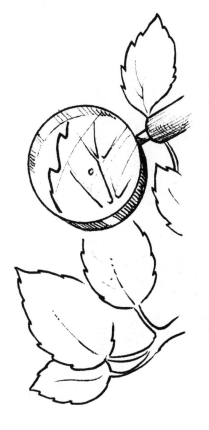

A butterfly lays an egg on a leaf. The egg is small enough to fit on the head of a pin.

Egg

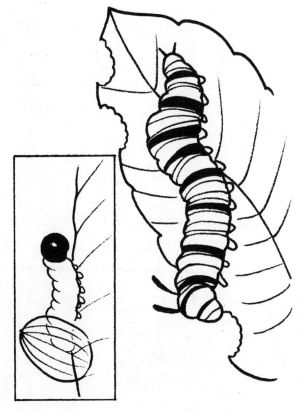

Hello, world! A caterpillar chews through the egg's shell. The caterpillar is tiny at first. But it eats lots of leaves and grows fast.

Caterpillar

The caterpillar hangs upside down from a twig. It grows a hard shell called a chrysalis (CRIS-uh-lis). It rests for about two weeks. Inside the chrysalis, the caterpillar is changing.

Chrysalis

Look! The caterpillar has turned into a butterfly! One day, the butterfly will lay an egg on a leaf. What do you think will happen then?

Butterfly

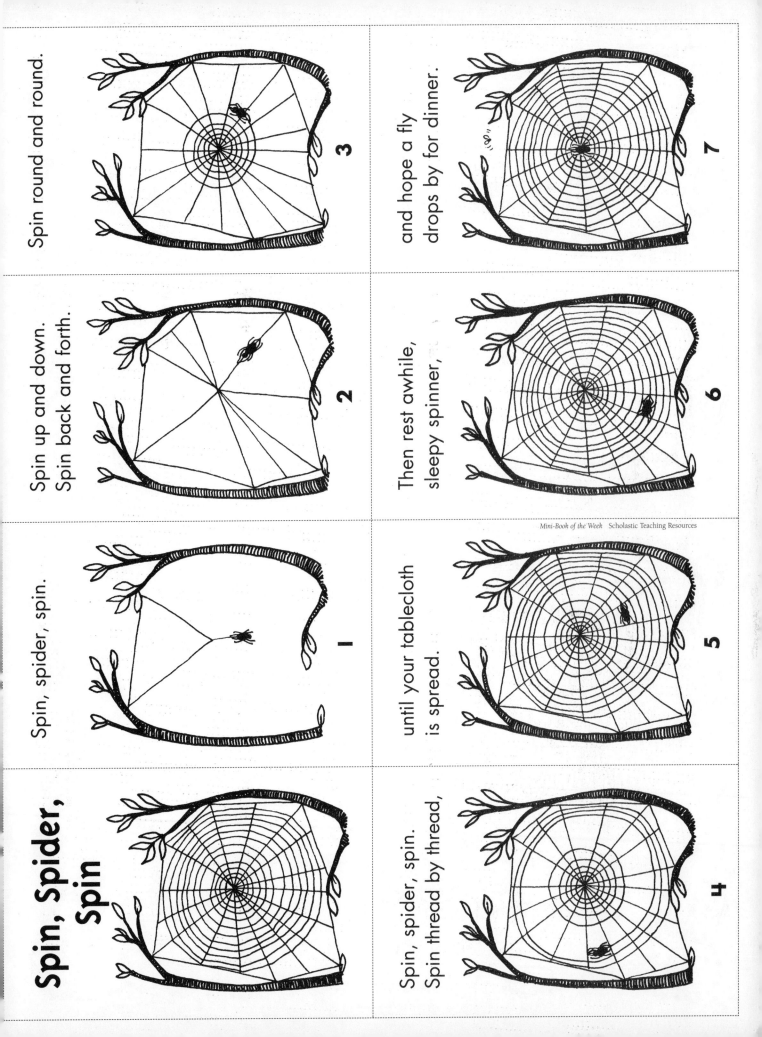

Spin, Spider, Spin

Spin, spider, spin.

1

Spin up and down.
Spin back and forth.

2

Spin round and round.

3

Spin, spider, spin.
Spin thread by thread,

4

until your tablecloth
is spread.

5

Then rest awhile,
sleepy spinner,

6

and hope a fly
drops by for dinner.

7

Mini-Book of the Week Scholastic Teaching Resources

Class Memory Book

Name: _____

Grade: _____

This year, I learned a lot of new things.
Some of the new things I learned were

_____

_____

_____

My favorite subject was _____.

1

We read a lot of books this year.
Some of my favorite books were

_____

_____

_____

_____

2

_____ is someone

from my school I will always remember.

I will remember this person because _____

_____

_____

_____

3

Our class shared many fun days together. One of the

best days was when _____

_____ .

4

The thing I am most proud of about this school year is

_____ .

5

Reading Time
Math

Summer's here. The school year's done.

1

5
+5
10

5
+6

Remember the things we learned,
the games we played,

3

Mini-Book of the Week   Scholastic Teaching Resources

My
Autograph
Book

Say good-bye to everyone.

2

Remember the fun we had ....

5

when you read the names
inside this book.

7

Mini-Book of the Week   Scholastic Teaching Resources

the books we read,
and the friends we made.

4

and the trips we took ....

6

When Summer Comes

When summer comes, you'll find me . . . .

1

sitting under my favorite tree,

2

watching fireflies flying free,

3

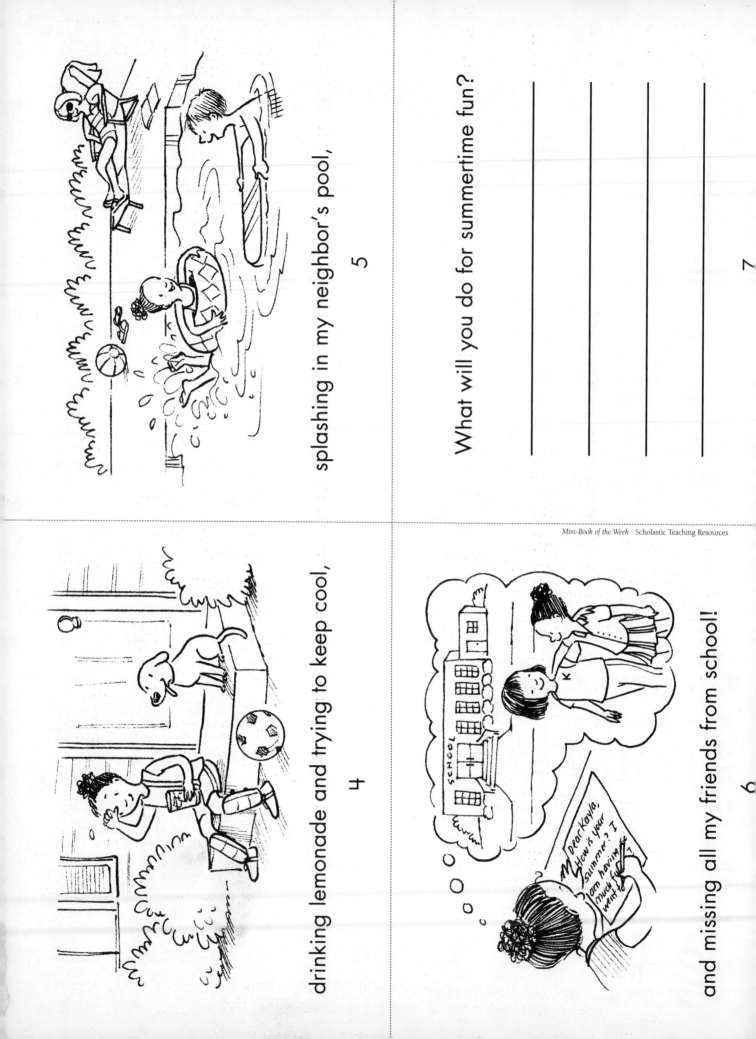

splashing in my neighbor's pool,

5

What will you do for summertime fun?

7

Mini-Book of the Week   Scholastic Teaching Resources

drinking lemonade and trying to keep cool,

4

and missing all my friends from school!

6